GLOWING PRA
REMARKABLE

"This is a moving, uplifting story . . . a metaphor for all our lives. It's practical, mystical and fun."
—**Susan Strasberg, actress and author**

"Compelling . . . Harricharan presents the reader with a fascinating mixture of personal experience and spiritual pilgrimage . . . and provides us with a glimpse of the Greater Reality."
—*True Psychic Inquirer*

"A personal spiritual odyssey reminiscent of Richard Bach's ILLUSIONS. Harricharan takes us along on his journey through life's often confusing and painful experiences. He shares the learning and understanding that comes when one begins to 'see' things right instead of trying to 'set' them right . . . He discovers a host of universal truths."
—*Psychic Guide*

"Fast-paced, totally absorbing and soul stirring! One of the very few books I was unable to put down until turning the last page. This is MUST reading!"
—**Foster Hibbard,**
President, Motivation Dynamics, Inc.

ABOUT THE AUTHOR

A prize-winning scholar and award-winning author, JOHN HARRICHARAN is a highly respected authority in the field of business evaluation and consultation services. Named "Businessman of the Week" and "Outstanding Young Man of America," he is a sought-after speaker and guest on numerous TV and radio broadcasts nationwide.

Berkley Books by John Harricharan

**WHEN YOU CAN WALK ON WATER, TAKE THE BOAT
MORNING HAS BEEN ALL NIGHT COMING**

When You Can Walk on Water, Take the Boat

John Harricharan

BERKLEY BOOKS, NEW YORK

This Berkley book contains the complete text
of the original edition. It has been
completely reset in a typeface designed for
easy reading and was printed from new film.

WHEN YOU CAN WALK ON WATER, TAKE THE BOAT

A Berkley Book / published by arrangement with
the author

PRINTING HISTORY
New World Publishing edition published 1986
Berkley edition / January 1991

ISBN: 0-425-12499-1

A BERKLEY BOOK ® TM 757,375
Berkley Books are published by The Berkley Publishing Group,
200 Madison Avenue, New York, New York 10016.
The name "Berkley" and the "B" logo
are trademarks belonging to Berkley Publishing Corporation.

PRINTED IN THE UNITED STATES OF AMERICA

10 9 8 7 6 5

Dedicated to
Malika Elizabeth and Jonathan Nian

SPECIAL THANKS

I am eternally grateful to my wife, Mardai, whose tremendous support made this work possible. Special thanks to Anita Bergen who untiringly shared the burdens of accuracy and coordination. And finally, my thanks to Sandra Matuschka and Cheryl Hudson for their much needed editorial assistance.

INTRODUCTION
by BRAD STEIGER

Somehow, I always think of my friend John Harricharan in an aura of mystery. The first time that I saw him he was seated in the audience as I was leading a large group of people through a guided meditation. I remember seeing this man looking intensely at me with his dark, compelling eyes and thinking: "Talk about synchronicity. I know that I have some kind of past life linkup with that guy!"

From that meeting onward, John and I have maintained a steady communication. Although we have been together in the physical for very limited periods of time, we always kept in touch through dreams, personal visions—and the more prosaic channel of the telephone.

Now, here is John writing a really nifty little book about metaphysical mysteries, and it all seems, somehow, very appropriate. I think one of the things I liked best about *When You Can Walk on Water, Take the Boat* (in addition to its magnificent title!) is the way John neatly blends universal truths with the strong sense of perspective of "one-who-has-been-there." You really get the feeling that Mr. Harricharan has paid some very heavy physical dues. Enlightenment came with some expensive price tags.

The series of ups and downs and crises and triumphs of the world of commerce coincide with a unique spiritual pilgrimage of soul in the higher realms. And throughout it all, the author keeps encouraging us to continue to learn and to grow. Because, he underscores, that is really what all the pain, chaos and confusion is actually trying to teach us: We chose to put on the fleshly clothes of earth to fulfill a mission of growth. All of this swirling energy around us can be interpreted as a quagmire of death and depression or as opportunities for life and learning.

The mysterious figures of Gideon and his fellow shadow-figures of . . . No, I don't want to give any part of this excellent extended allegory away. That wouldn't be fair to you, the reader. After all, I was able to participate with John in an exciting sense of discovery. I shouldn't cheat you of any of the fun and profit of your own thrill of exploration at the hands of a very skilled and sympathetic guide.

Thank you, John, for your willingness to share a hunk of your inner self with each of us!

Brad Steiger
Scottsdale, Arizona

PREFACE

The question asked most of me by those who read this manuscript before publication was, "Is it true?" My answer was the age-old question, "What is Truth?" This is a book about you and me and others of our world. The ancient truths are as old as the hills, yet, they shine ever so radiantly with newness whenever they are rediscovered.

It is no accident that you have picked up this book. Perhaps, it is by "divine appointment" that we meet in these pages and explore again the meaning of life. Perhaps, in the exploration and adventures that follow, you would rediscover and realize that you are a being of infinite power and potential, only limited by your own beliefs about yourself.

What follows will mean different things to different people. For some, it will be a lovely otherworldly adventure but for others, it will be a powerful re-awakening.

Life is lived from within and one can never be hurt by what appears to be happening outside. You can change circumstances if you so desire. Your only purpose in life is to make choices. Once the choice is made, the entire universe moves to bring into fruition that which you chose.

Read then, with an open mind and let yourself ask you questions. Many of these things you already know but may have only forgotten. Let us remember together the true nature of our being.

John Harricharan

When You Can Walk on Water, Take the Boat

CHAPTER
1

It was evening time. Not completely dark but with traces of day still remaining. Everyone had left the office and I was there, all alone, completing the few tasks that remain at the end of any day. It is not my nature to work late, but this day was somewhat different. Mixed with a feeling of accomplishment was the frustration and anger of not having done all I would have liked to do.

My office was at the end of the building, overlooking a parking lot. The lot was empty save for my little car, which appeared to be waiting so patiently. Always it seemed to be waiting for me, never complaining, always nearby. "Time to leave," I thought. "I am already late." If there was one consolation, it was that there would be no traffic at this hour.

3

Glancing through the window as I reached for my attache case, I noticed a blue car a few spaces removed from mine. The hood was up, and it seemed as if someone was trying to fix something. It was not unusual for cars to limp into our parking lot with some problem. I went down the stairs to the main door, set the night alarm and walked out of the building.

The blue car was still there with the hood raised. I walked toward it with the idea of seeing whether I could be of any assistance. Through the window in the dim light, I saw a bearded face smiling at me. "What took you so long? I thought you might have changed your mind," he said. The nerve of the man, I thought. A total stranger, and he wanted to know what took me so long. Ingratitude bothers me. It struck me as somewhat strange, however, that he seemed to have been expecting me. But I dismissed the thought.

"Try the motor once more," I shouted. He did, and it immediately sprang to life and kept running with a beautiful purr as if nothing had been the matter with it all this time. The bearded one got out of his car, walked up to me, stretched out his hand and said, "Hi! It's good to see you again for the first time. My name is Gideon."

"Hello, Mr. Gideon, it's good to meet you," I stammered, shaking his outstretched hand. "My name is John."

"Yes, I know" he said. This took me by surprise. I had never seen the man before. He was

4

dressed in everyday clothes and appeared to be somewhere between the ages of 50 and 60. He was not tall. His hair was jet black and neatly combed with one lock falling idly over his right brow. The beard, which was as black as his hair, was full and trimmed, but his eyes were his most noticeable feature. Even in the dim light from the street lamp, one could see those piercing orbs as if they had a story to tell. Such determined eyes, and yet, such kindness in them. Although I noticed all these things in a split second, I kept staring at him all the while.

He smiled. "Beautiful weather we're having," he said.

I nodded. I couldn't have cared less for the weather at that moment. "How do you know my name?" I quickly asked.

"Oh, I guessed. Most everyone is Jim or John or Ron or Tom." He said it matter-of-factly, but there was something in his voice that seemed to suggest that he really knew my name. Perhaps this was one of those set-ups I had heard so much about recently. Perhaps he was intent on doing me harm—stealing or something. I had the greatest urge to leave that spot and remove myself from him as fast as possible, but the kindness in those eyes held me there.

"I see that you are alarmed, concerned about your safety," he said, seeming to pull the very thoughts out of my head. "No need to fear. I thank you for assisting me with the car. I feared no one would come at this hour, but there you

5

were. People these days are so afraid of everything, of each other, of the dark, yes, even of themselves. My gratitude to you, John."

I figured that he had to be lying since I hardly did anything to assist him in the starting of his car. It just appeared to me that the motor started the second that I told him to try it again. Anyway, I said, "I didn't do anything, but you are welcome nevertheless."

"Perhaps we shall meet again soon," he said as I moved toward my car.

"Perhaps," I muttered, thinking of how unlikely that would be. He waved as I stepped into my car and drove out of the parking lot.

By now it was really dark, and my wife and children would be wondering where I was and whether I was stranded on the road. It was the normal, short drive, no more than 15 minutes or so before I pulled up to the mailbox at the bottom of my driveway. As is my custom everyday, I collected the mail and started driving up to the garage. The driveway is long and curving and the thought occurred to me to make preparations for snow removal in the winter time. It was far from winter and yet my tired mind was already thinking of it.

I wondered about Gideon but brushed the thought away, since I felt I had done my good deed for the day and probably would never see him again. There were more important things to do now, like dinner, walking the dog and finally, taking out the garbage. Dinner and then walking the dog would be pleasant. "Rajah," my collie, was a spirited, friendly animal, and a little run with him would do both of us some good.

As I walked into the house, mail in one hand and attache case in the other, my little boy, Jonathan, was waiting for me. Only three years old, he had no concept of time and so was not too surprised to see me at that late hour. Laying aside the mail and attache case, I picked up Jonathan and went into the kitchen. My wife, Mardai, and daughter, Malika, greeted me warmly. The aroma of slowly simmering chicken stew made me realize how hungry I was.

"What kept you so late today, John?" my wife asked as we sat down to dinner.

"Oh, nothing much. Just helped a fellow get his car started." Dinner over, I took care of the other chores, assisted in putting the children to bed and discussed some of the day's activities with my wife. Finally, we watched a short show on television and then I read for a little while. I love to read but there never seems to be enough time to do so. I generally am reading at least five books at different stages, going from one to the other until I complete them all. It is certainly not the best way to read books, but I do get through them.

We decided to turn in, and only then did I feel the fatigue of the day. Reflecting on my strange meeting with Gidcon, I fell asleep.

CHAPTER

It is my habit to wake up very early in the morning. I am one of those ridiculous fellows who finds it almost impossible to sleep late. Whether I go to bed at eight o'clock in the evening or two in the morning, I still get up by five or six. This morning being no exception, I was up and ready to go by six-thirty. I said good-bye to my family and drove the short distance to the office.

A breathtaking morning it was indeed. The rays of the sun streaming through the windows of the car warmed my very being and made me want to sing for joy. Actually, "sing" is not the word to describe the sounds I make in the attempt, but in the car, no one hears and there is the feeling of safety in that private cubicle.

Except on those rare occasions when a driver pulls up at a stop light, looks at me quizzically and drives away, I am not conscious of the quality of my own singing.

I pulled into the parking lot half expecting to see the blue car of the night before. Of course, it was not there. "What a strange man," I thought, "I feel as if I know him or have seen him someplace before. Perhaps it was at a conference or a convention." It was not long, however, before I was caught up in the day's activities.

Things were not going too well for the company. We had designed and built a portable device that was of use to printers and photographers. It was an excellent machine, capable of recycling the valuable chemicals from their waste processing solutions. Although we had received a large number of compliments about it, sales were not increasing as fast as we had expected and, as everyone knows, compliments do not pay the bills. I had built up an excellent management team and we were expanding our horizons. But still, at times, I felt so alone in what I was doing.

The sound of the ringing phone woke me up from my reverie. It was our plant manager calling to inform me that an entire production line had to be shut down immediately. "Do whatever you can. I will be over shortly," was all that I could say. Another phone call. The voice of my secretary heralded the type of calls I was getting. "It is Mr. Abe Ludic," she said. "Do you

12

want me to tell him that you will call him later?"

"No, I'll take it," I replied.

She switched the call to my line and for the next five minutes I explained to Mr. Ludic why a past due bill remained unpaid.

Telephone calls for the purpose of collecting past due payments coupled with the company's financial situation were enough to drive me to distraction. We had even applied recently for a substantial loan from a local bank only to have the banker laugh at us.

Whenever I feel like becoming depressed, there is a game that I play with myself. It always seems to work. I stop doing everything and say to myself, "Now, John, since you like to do everything well, take the next ten or fifteen minutes and become as depressed as possible. Wallow in your misery. Think how terrible things are and how the entire world is against you. Note how everyone whom you know goes out of his way to make your life unpleasant. Think of how very unfortunate you are. Now, as soon as the second hand on your watch reaches twelve, start." When the second hand reaches twelve, I try to become as miserable as possible. Within a few minutes I am laughing so hard at the silly nature of my thoughts that the depression vanishes.

Somehow or other, I was able to make it through to lunch time. We were able to get the production line back on stream and Mr. Ludic agreed to wait for another week. I do not normally eat lunch. In fact I could go without breakfast and lunch without ever feeling uncomfortable. Today was no exception. There was a strong urge in me, however, to leave the office and go on one of my usual short walks. It would be refreshing, I thought, so I went.

I had gone quite a few blocks when I decided to return by an alternate route which would take me by a quaint little restaurant. It was a demanding morning, so I had taken a longer walk than usual. As I approached a corner, I had the persistent feeling that there was an appointment that I may have forgotten. I have been known to forget appointments before, so instead of returning to the office, I figured that I would use the public phone in the little restaurant, call my office and check whether or not there was an appointment.

I quickly walked up to the restaurant, opened the door and walked in looking for a phone. Seeing one on the other side of the room, I went over and, after inserting the proper coin, dialed my office. I inquired about whether I had an appointment and was assured that I did not. I breathed a sigh of relief, but still had the strange feeling that I had to meet someone. I decided to have a quick lunch since I was already in the restaurant.

I walked over to the hostess who looked at me, smiled sweetly and said, "Mr. H., please follow me." As I followed her across the dining room, I thought how flattering it was that she recognized me. It is a small northeastern town that I live in. It is an even smaller town that I work in. Almost everybody knows one another. She led me to a table over by the far corner near a window. I thanked her and even before I was properly seated, she said, "Your other party will be here soon."

"My other party?" I asked. I was surprised, since no one, not even myself, knew that I would be stopping by this restaurant. She saw my surprise, looked around and said, "Oh, here he is now. Enjoy your lunch."

Up to my table, walked Gideon. Ignoring my questioning gaze, he seated himself, smiled and said, "Fine day it is."

"Fine day it is, but what are you doing here?" I asked.

"Hope you don't mind my joining you."

"Of course not. But I certainly did not think that I was going to see you again so soon." I was becoming somewhat confused. First the incident in the parking lot, then the strange urge to walk by the restaurant, followed by my decision to have lunch and finally meeting Gideon again. "Did you make reservations or plan to be here for lunch today?"

"Yes, I made the reservations for both of us."

"How did you know that I'd be here? Even I didn't know."

"Just had a feeling. You have such feelings at times, don't you? The phone rings and you know who is calling. You think of someone you haven't

15

heard from in years and you receive a letter from that person. Just had a hunch that you would be here and I took the chance."

"I was thinking about you. I wondered whether I was ever again going to see the bearded man whose car was stuck in our parking lot. By the way, is everything fixed now? Does it run well?"

"Runs better than ever." His eyes seemed even more piercing than in our previous encounter. They seemed to probe the very depths of my mind, leaving me to feel that I could hide nothing from him. "Didn't think you would make it again this time," he continued, as if speaking to himself.

"Pardon me?"

"Oh, nothing. I talk to myself sometimes."

"Well, since you are here, I'll say that it's good to see you. Let's have a quick bite, since I must be back at the office shortly."

"One of your problems, John, is that you hurry too much. Yesterday in the parking lot you were in a rush. Today at lunch you're in a hurry again. Take some time to enjoy life. Everyone has the same measure of time, you know. Twenty-four hours a day. It's what you do with your time that's important."

I really didn't think that I needed to be preached to today but I wanted to be as polite as possible. "It's easy to say that," I replied, "I have responsibilities, you know. A business to run.

16

Things to do. Sometimes the burden of it all gets to me."

"Only if you let it. And everyone has responsibilities. Do you know that the word responsibility means 'ability to respond'? Do you have a business to run or do you let the business run you?"

For someone I was meeting for only the second time, he certainly had a lot to say about me. A good philosophical discussion, however, always brightens my day, and besides, there was some truth in what he had said. "You seem to have things nice and easy," I said. "Where do you work and what do you do anyway?"

A strange look came into those dark eyes. "Actually I am a trouble shooter," he said, "a jack-of-all-trades, if you will. What you would probably call a consultant for my company, if you know what I mean."

"And your company?"

"It's called G & M Enterprises, Inc. It's not the car company, you know. I'm sure that you have never heard of it."

"Can't say that I have. Is it a large corporation?"

"To a certain extent. Very diverse. In many countries. World headquarters in the Big City. Branch offices throughout the country."

"What do they make or do?"

"Somewhat of a service company, more or less."

Sensing his reluctance to give more information and not wanting to be rude I asked, "Are you on vacation now?"

"No. Actually I'm on assignment. I'll be in this area for a little while."

"Do you live around here?"

"Not really. Just passing through. After completion of my current assignment, I'll be on the road again."

"Well, I hope they give you a better car," I said with a laugh, remembering his problems of the evening before. He smiled, and changed the conversation back to my work. "So things are not going too well with your business?" he asked.

"We've been struggling for a long time, a real long time, Gideon. There are times when we think we see light at the end of the tunnel but, more often than not, it's a freight train. It's tough."

"Why struggle? A swimmer does not struggle with the water. He flows with it, using it as a means of reaching his goal. Don't struggle, just follow the flow."

The restaurant was mostly empty now. We had finished our simple lunch in between our conversation. Only two tables across from us were occupied. I glanced at my watch. It was time to go. But my strange friend was not ready to leave. He gave me the impression that he wanted to tell me something. Again, I had that sense of foreboding—not quite foreboding but almost like I was getting into things for which I was not ready nor prepared. I paid the bill. He offered to pay his share but I refused it. He thanked me and got up.

"Do you have a business card?" I asked. He reached into his pocket, pulled out a card and handed it to me. "Thank you. I must say good-bye now and go back to that unpleasant job I have," I said.

"Be grateful that you have a job to go to," he replied. We walked to the door and went outside. I hoped that he was not setting me up for something. I am somewhat of a pushover when I like someone, and I was beginning to take a liking to this stranger.

As we said good-bye, I told him that I hoped we would meet again soon. He nodded and said, "It really is a small world. I will see you soon." He turned, waved and left.

I slowly walked back to the office. All during lunch I felt an aura of kindness and, strangely enough, power around Gideon. Now, back in the sunlight, the apparent mystery seemed to dissolve.

The afternoon passed smoothly without as many difficulties as the morning. Several times I glanced through the window into the parking lot where I had first seen Gideon. Perhaps we would meet again.

There was going to be a little dinner party at my house in the evening. Just a few friends and neighbors getting together to enjoy one another's company. It was beginning to get dark. Possibly a storm was on the way, I thought. You never can tell with the weather these days. I decided to leave early to reach home before the rain started.

I was about to pull into my driveway when all the driveway lights went out. I thought perhaps that the impending storm had something to do with it. Then the storm broke. Such fury of wind and rain I have rarely seen. The rain was a sheet of white water interspersed with the reflection of brilliant flashes of lightning. The sound of thunder reminded one of the legends of the gods that lived on Mount Olympus hurling thunderbolts at their enemies. I could hardly see as I drove up the driveway, got out of the car and rushed into the house getting drenched in the few seconds it took me to do so.

All was dark inside except for the areas lit by a few candles my wife had found. Our guests arrived and we made the best of a poor situation. We ate by candlelight and marvelled at the many faces of nature.

"It seems really strange to me, John," one of the guests remarked.

"What seems strange?" I asked.

"The fury and nature of this storm. I just telephoned a neighbor down the street and he said that it didn't rain there."

"Not raining there? A few blocks away?" I was extremely surprised.

"And all their lights are on," he continued.

It was strange to see a storm that occurred in only a few square blocks. For no apparent reason

I thought of Gideon. Immediately there was the largest flash of lightning and all our lights came back on. We discussed the storm for a little while. I seemed to connect it with something having to do with Gideon. Yet, that made no sense.

CHAPTER
3

CHAPTER

3

Two weeks had passed since I last saw Gideon. Things at the office seemed to be a little worse. Business was not getting any better. Our newly invented device was not selling as we had expected. We were fast approaching a financial crisis again. It began to seem as though in the past few years, my life had been a journey from crisis to crisis with only a brief time in between. Then, unexpectedly, I had to make a trip to the Midwest.

A potential account we had been nurturing for the past six months suddenly exhibited tremendous interest in our product. It would be a short trip, just two days. All travel and hotel arrangements made, it soon was time to leave. The ride to the airport was not an unpleasant one. It is a rather modern airport, and I was pleased to be leaving from there.

No matter how many times I've flown, there is always a sense of excitement as I approach an airport. The sound of the jets generates thoughts of faraway places that intrigue me, but this was a business trip and all my thoughts had to be concentrated on the matter at hand.

After a pleasant flight, it was but a short cab ride to my hotel. I would be ready in the morning for my meeting with Mr. Seymour, the head of the interested company. I had never met Mr. Seymour before but hoped that he would receive my proposal in a favorable manner. A good night's rest and I would be brilliant, I thought. As I was filling in the necessary registration form, the lady behind the desk smiled and said, "We have a message for you, Mr. H." I opened the note. It stated simply that M. Tarkas would meet me later. Perhaps it was Mr. Seymour's idea to send someone to meet me.

I went to my room, unpacked my small overnight bag and took a quick shower. Then I phoned home to let everyone know that I had arrived safely. When it was time for dinner, I went down to the dining room. As I was walking across the lobby, a lady stepped up to me and said, "Hi! I'm Marla Tarkas. You're John!"

"Should I know you?" I asked, momentarily startled.

"Gideon told me you would be here and asked

that I give you as much help as you are willing to receive."

Ah, here we go, I thought. Gideon again. And I hadn't seen him in weeks. Who was this woman anyway? How had Gideon known about my trip? Perhaps he had called my office and someone had mentioned it to him. But my secretary never gives out that sort of information. I must admit that I was a giant question mark as I stood there looking at Marla.

She smiled at me sweetly. "May I join you for dinner? We'll talk more then." I nodded and we went to the dining room. When we were seated, I looked at Marla with evident discomfort.

She was beautiful but had a distant look on her face as if deep in thought. Her eyes were blue and her hair seemed to reflect a golden glow. She appeared to be perhaps 25 or so, but certainly not more than 30.

"How long have you know Gideon?" I asked.

"Oh, for ages," she said, smiling.

"I haven't seen him in weeks. And I really don't know Gideon that well. Had lunch with him once. Are you good friends?"

"He's one of my closest friends. We've been through a lot together."

"I wonder how Gideon knew of my trip," I said, hoping that Marla would shed some light on this. She responded, "Gideon knows many things and has his own ways of finding out."

I rolled this around in my mind for a few

27

seconds, making no sense of it. Then I asked her, "Do you work around here?"

"Not too far away."

"What's the name of your company?"

"You probably never heard of it, but it's called G & M Enterprises, Inc. I'm in the PR Department."

"Isn't that the same company Gideon works for?"

"He's in a different department, though."

It was now all clear to me. Gideon and Marla knew each other because they worked for the same company. Gideon found out, one way or another, about my trip, called Marla and asked her to assist me. He was trying to repay the favor of my helping him in the parking lot and buying him lunch. It was so simple now. Yet, why go to such extremes to repay a small favor?

The rest of dinner was spent telling Marla about my meeting with Mr. Seymour in the morning and the large contract my company hoped to land, discussing the state of the economy, and so forth. When we were through with dinner, she insisted on paying the bill. I objected, but she would not listen. "You are my guest, John," she said, simply.

As we left the table, she wished me success at my meeting the next day. I thanked her politely for dinner and for the time she had spent with me. Then she said something about my receiving a phone call later in the evening and was gone before I could question her. I was not expecting any phone calls and was puzzled. Perhaps, I thought, Marla herself would call later.

I went back to my room, changed into my pajamas, and read for a while. Whenever I travel, I always take along a few good books. This trip was no exception, so I stayed up late reading and waiting for the phone call Marla told me about.

It was getting late and I needed a good night's rest to be fresh and ready to go in the morning. No phone call yet. Perhaps I had misunderstood Marla. Thinking of what the following day would bring, I put away my book, turned off the lights and fell asleep. And as I slept, I dreamed.

In my dream, I went to a City near to the one in which I lived. There was an appointment I had to keep, so after locating the building where I was supposed to be, I went in. Behind a long desk sat a young lady who I assumed was the receptionist. She looked up at me and before I could tell her my purpose for being there, she said, "Please wait. I must leave for a few minutes," and she was gone. While I waited for her return, the phone rang. I hoped that it would stop, at least until she returned, but it kept on and on as if determined to have me answer it.

I could not ignore the ringing any longer so I finally picked up the receiver, if only to tell the other party that the receptionist would be back later. "Hello," I said. A friendly voice on the other end spoke, "Hi! Good morning. May I speak with Mr. Seymour, please?"

"I'm sorry sir. The person who answers the phone just stepped away from her desk for a short while. In fact, I am awaiting her return," I said.

"Please, could you ask her when she returns to give Mr. Seymour a message for me?" he asked.

"Why certainly, " I said, most anxious to help.

"Please ask her to tell Mr. Seymour that Godfrey called. I have been talking with the Wittersham account and they are extremely interested. Mr. Wittersham himself is on his way over and will sign all necessary papers." I agreed to convey his message for which he thanked me and hung up. When the receptionist returned, I gave her the message. She then asked me to follow her and we went into an office where a distinguished looking gentleman was sitting at his desk. He rose and introduced himself. "I am Seymour," he said in a kindly voice. "Please sit."

Mr. Seymour told me that his company would buy our products if one of his largest accounts, the Wittersham Company, agreed to distribute them. He told me a little about Mr. Wittersham and how the Wittersham Company grew from a small start to one of the largest in its field. Wittersham, it seemed, was from the old school, conservative, had little patience and was a hard man to deal with. The only topic that he was ever interested in was the sea and he would spend hours talking about it.

Mr. Seymour was pleased that I had come. "Make sure you tell Wittersham about your early days by the ocean," he said, and all of a sudden the dream ended and I was awake in bed. It was a most vivid dream and thinking about it kept me awake for almost the remainder of the night.

Finally, it was morning and I got up and prepared for my meeting with Mr. Seymour. After breakfast, I took a cab to his office. All the buildings were tall and clustered together in what appeared to be the main commercial area of the city. I paid my fare and walked into the building where Seymour's office was located. Without much waiting, I was ushered in to see him. The expression on my face was one of pure astonishment when I discovered that the real Mr. Seymour and the Mr. Seymour of my dream were exactly alike in physical features. I had never seen this man before and the coincidence seemed remarkable.

We talked for a while about my company's new product. He would be willing to do some business with us, he said, but that would depend on one of his largest distributors. There was a knock at the door and an assistant came in and whispered to Mr. Seymour. Seymour smiled, looked at me and said, "I am told that old James Wittersham just arrived and he is insisting on seeing me immediately." He turned to the assistant, who was still standing there, and asked her to show Mr. Wittersham in.

At first glance, Wittersham hardly seemed friendly. He gave a quick nod when I was introduced and started talking immediately.

"Look now, Seymour. I don't have much time. Tell me about this thing you want me to handle."

The whole scene appeared to be a reflection of my dream last night. I finally grew brave enough to look Mr. Wittersham directly in the eye and say, "Sir, perhaps I could be of some help. I'm from the company that manufactures the machine we're discussing. If you could give me five minutes of your time, I will explain why our machine is so good."

"Good? I don't want good! I want the best."

"I was being modest. It's the best out on the market."

Wittersham was a study in marble. Deep lines creased his face as he looked from me to Seymour and said, "Let's get on with it."

The next few minutes I spent explaining all the benefits of our product. Wittersham appeared to be utterly unimpressed. Finally, in exasperation and in an effort to clutch at straws, I remembered my dream about Wittersham and the sea and concluded, "So you see, Mr. Wittersham, we make an excellent product. Incidentally, I wish you would visit our facilities on the East Coast. Some lovely restaurants by the sea." He quickly looked at me and asked, "By the sea? Do you go there often?"

"Oh yes!" I responded. "I love to go down to the sea."

"I wish we had the ocean closer to us," he said. Pursuing the only possibility afforded me, I continued, "I was born not too far from the ocean. I spent 18 years of my life a stone's throw from the mighty Atlantic. I'd waken every morning to the sound of breakers. I'd watch the sea change from a silvery white in the morning to a deep dark blue in the late afternoon." Seymour was looking at me and I could feel the frustration in his look as we discussed the sea. But the change on Wittersham's face was amazing. Gone was the scowl and he was smiling.

"We must speak more about the sea one of these days," said Wittersham, "I myself am an old salt." Turning to Seymour, Wittersham continued, "Seymour, I'll be happy to have my company distribute your machines." He then got up abruptly, said good-bye, and left.

I could hardly contain myself. After so many months we had finally landed one of the largest accounts in this business. Seymour would now take on our product because his largest distributor wanted it. The dark clouds of business were lifting and my spirit had already taken wings. I couldn't wait to tell them about it back home.

Seymour and I continued our conversation but it was now in a lighter vein. We talked about boyhood days when I stood on the shores of the Atlantic and looked as far as the eye could see. How the passing of tramp steamers with smoky stacks would carry my thoughts to distant shores. How the tall ships with billowing, white sails would conjure up visions of mystic climes and far-off places. I told him of the many times I stood by a tree on the beach wondering if there were other little boys standing on other shores looking out and wondering, just as I was doing.

I told him that it was the song of the sea that lured me from my birthplace, that led me through tropic isles with balmy breezes and finally set me down in the northeast portion of the United States. He smiled as I mentioned that the song of the sea and the thought of the tradewinds still strongly call to me, somewhat like the singing of the sirens of old to a tired Ulysses.

Finally it was time to go. Seymour agreed to have all the necessary documents signed and sent to me within a few days. He promised to work very closely with us to make the project a success. I took my leave of him and returned to the hotel. It had been an exciting morning.

Marla was waiting for me in the lobby. "I trust that you had a productive morning," she said with a quick smile.

"Most productive," I replied, and as an afterthought mentioned that no one had called me last evening.

"Of course you got the call."

"No! Nobody called me last night," I insisted.

"Did you not receive a call for a Mr. Seymour? And was not a Mr. Wittersham discussed? And did not the call contain important information which you used during your meeting today? Have you forgotten your dream?"

I almost fell through the floor. I had told no one about my dream, not that there was anyone

34

to tell anyway. Yet Marla knew about it. In fact, it seemed that she knew exactly what dream I was going to have that night. I stared at her with awe. She seemed in some ways so similar to Gideon, especially in the way she said things. What manner of people were these, I wondered. Noticing my discomfiture, she calmly said, "Don't be alarmed. You will understand more soon. Your flight leaves at 6 p.m. so I'll pick you up at 5 p.m. This way, we'll have enough time to get you to your plane." Before I could answer, she turned and was gone.

Puzzled and intrigued by the turn of events, I went to my room, packed my things, lay down for a while to think over the events of the day and promptly fell asleep, thus missing lunch. When I awoke, it was almost 5 p.m. so I collected my things and went down to the lobby to await Marla's arrival. I tried to put out of my mind any thoughts about her and Gideon and their strange ways.

Marla was punctual. We made it to the airport in record time. In spite of the rush hour traffic, it seemed almost as if the vehicles moved out of the way for us. Before saying good-bye, Marla mentioned that she was extremely happy to have been of some assistance to me, that any friend of Gideon's was a friend of hers and that it would not be too long before all of us met again. I thanked her, wished her well, and boarded my flight.

Much as I tried to keep Marla and Gideon out

of my mind, they stayed with me and raised a thousand questions during the flight. I finally managed to engross myself in one of the in-flight magazines, knowing that in a few hours I would be home.

CHAPTER
4

O n my way to the office the following morning, I could not help but reflect on the events of the past few days. Without a doubt, the trip was an amazing success. I wondered whether Mr. Wittersham would have agreed to distribute our products had it not been for the conversation about the sea, which he loved. And how would I have ever thought about talking of the ocean had it not been for the dream I had the night before the meeting. Again, these thoughts raised questions about Gideon and Marla. The more I thought about it, the more complex it seemed to me—a simple man, not concerned most times with complex situations.

The sound of a car horn woke me from my reverie. It was an old Volkswagen passing me on the left. I briefly wondered why the driver sounded his horn since I was already in the right lane. As it passed me, however, I noticed the word "GIDEON" on its license plate. I almost ran into a telephone post. How odd, I thought.

Within minutes of my arrival at the office, the telephone rang. It was the private line. The sound startled me since it was still only seven in the morning and I was not expecting any calls so early. Only three people had the number of my private line: one was my wife and the other two were extremely close friends. I picked up the hand-set. It was Gideon.

"How did you get this number?" I asked.

"Shouldn't you first ask how I'm doing?" he answered.

Dutifully I asked, "How are you Gideon?" followed quickly by, "How did you get this number?"

"I'm sure you have a lot of questions and that's why I called. Listen, John, we'll meet in the park at lunchtime and I'll explain everything." He hung up. As abruptly as that.

At first, I thought I would ignore the incident and stay as far away from these people as possible, but curiosity got the better of me and I decided to see him.

It was almost noon when I left the office for the short walk to the park. Gideon, hopefully, would be there and would provide an explanation for some of the things that had occurred. It was a lovely, sunny day. I felt very much like sitting

40

under a tree and practicing changing the shape of clouds. I found it both exciting and relaxing at the same time. You pick a small cloud at first and then try to mold it in your mind into various vapory sculptures. As you become more adept at it, you choose larger and larger clouds. You may even want to vaporize them entirely or create new ones where there weren't any before. It is amazing how easily it works.

Arriving at the park, I picked a spot under a large oak tree, where there was a bench. I sat down and waited for Gideon while looking at the birds and squirrels. It was peaceful and, strangely, almost other-worldly beautiful. A blue jay was pecking at a piece of bread someone had dropped, and the wind ran races through the growing grass. Except for me, there wasn't anyone else in the park. A voice interrupted, "Hope I haven't kept you waiting long." I turned around and there was Gideon. "Funny I didn't see you arrive," I said.

He was dressed this time in a sailor's outfit, as if he had been out sailing. He sat next to me on the bench and started biting into an apple he had brought.

"Aren't you hungry?" he asked.

"No, I am going to skip lunch today."

"Are you sure? I have another apple you can have."

"No, thank you."

We both sat for a while in silence before I blurted out, "How did you know about my trip?

41

How did you get my telephone number and anyway, who is Marla?"

"Slowly, John. One question at a time. You have been wondering about how I know certain things. Let me tell you. I know many things. You know them, too. However, you just don't remember them. Some of us remember much more than others. Think again of how many things you have known without ever being able to figure out how you knew them."

"Is that all? Are you a psychic or something like that? You see things happen before they do? I know a lady who could do that."

"That, I am, too. But much more is involved. It is one way of explaining it."

"You are more than a psychic? Who are you? What are you?"

He looked at me quizzically with a semi-pleased expression on his bearded face. "Of course I am more than a psychic," he said, "I am Gideon. I am who I am. I am I."

I had come here for answers and not to listen to riddles. Those were answers a schoolboy could give. I was determined, more than ever, to get to the bottom of this. "Who is Marla Tarkas?" I asked.

"Did you like her? I hoped you would. An extremely fine energy form she is."

"And an extremely fine physical form, too. But who is she? What is this that you people are involved in? Is this a cult?"

He was much more serious now. "No, John,

not a cult as you would think. There are some of us who are in certain types of work that are different from the types you have been accustomed to. We are joined together by bonds that go back into what is called eternity. Marla is such a one. So am I and so, of course, are you."

I stopped him right there. "It's fine for you and Marla to be . . . well . . . whatever you are or want to be, but leave me out of this." I was becoming somewhat annoyed and uncomfortable with his answers. He continued speaking.

"You know me as Gideon. And that I am. But a name does not tell much. I am what is called, a 'helper of mankind.' I come from way before your time and go far beyond your guess. I come from anytime and anyplace and could go anywhere and anywhen."

I sat glued to the wooden bench. I had known that he was strange, but not this strange. I never really took him seriously before, but now, he was dead serious. I did wonder on occasion how he knew things about me and my work that I had not told him about. I had heard about such people before. I had not discounted the possibility of meeting one, in fact, I had hoped that I would someday. Yet, when one sits next to you on a park bench, the initial reaction is to run away as fast as possible. Sitting there with him, I felt an aura of tremendous power around him and thought that I should look at this encounter a little more seriously than I was doing.

"You speak as if you are from another world,

Gideon. You seem to also have strange abilities and powers. Why are you spending so much time with me? What do you want from me?"

"My abilities are no stranger than yours or anyone else's. They may appear strange to you because you do not understand them. When you understand natural law, nothing is strange, nothing is a miracle. I have been around assisting others for ages. Or better yet, throughout time. There is an old earth saying that goes, 'When the student is ready, the teacher will appear.' You're ready, so here I am."

"Who? Me, a student? I wasn't looking for a teacher. I have had my share of teachers. I don't want to take any more exams. As it is these days, I am already being tested to the utmost. Teachers and students imply tests."

"So you think that you have learned everything and have no need of a teacher? If you are so brilliant, how come your financial empire is falling apart? Listen. All life is an examination, a learning and testing experience, if you will. You examine and test yourself constantly. A little help now and then wouldn't hurt, you know. There are things I still can teach you. No, let me rephrase. There are things I could lead you to learn. Things I could assist you to remember."

Part of me really wanted to believe him. The other part was the scientific, analytical part of me which is the same for everyone. That part said that he was crazy. And yet, I have seen few men who appeared to be more sane than he.

44

"Show me something, a small miracle or so, and I'll believe what you are saying."

"Believe and I will show you. You have things reversed, John. I see we have much work to do."

In a quick change of direction, I asked, "Where is your car? Where are you parked?"

"There are other ways of travelling. I don't really need a car."

Again, he was lying, I thought. The first time I met him, he was in a car.

As if reading my thoughts, he said, "When you saw me the first time, I did have a vehicle. I needed something to catch your attention. So the car, the broken engine, the lifted hood . . . all props, all effects for your sake. You wouldn't have stopped and talked with me any other way."

All this in such a short time was becoming too much for me. As I mentioned earlier, it had always been my desire to meet one such as he. In books and dreams I had come across some, but, here and now, in a park in a small town? This was a different matter. And why did he choose me? He still hadn't answered that to my satisfaction. I was quiet for a few moments.

Gideon continued, "I have known you for eons, for millennia. You are a challenge to me. One part of you accepts totally and with full understanding, all that I am saying. Then there is the other part of you that sees only with eyes and hears only with ears. That part tries to rationalize and compromise various situations. You are a man of many parts, Mr. H."

Gideon's reference to knowing me for ages was a surprise but I had read about such things before and chose not to pursue it at this point. Not being in a big hurry to go back to the office, I thought that I would listen to a little more of what he had to say.

He spoke of seeing with the third eye and of hearing with the inner ear. That all life forms were connected to one another by invisible ties. That the universe was like a spider's web, where thought or action in one area affected the entire fabric. I listened, fascinated by the new possibilities he brought to my mind. Finally, he said, "It was good seeing you again, John. We will continue our conversation at a later date. Meanwhile, keep an open mind. I bid you a fond adieu."

I looked at him and then at my watch. When I glanced up again, he was gone. It could not have been more than a second later, yet he was nowhere to be seen. Perhaps I had fallen asleep on the park bench and dreamed it all. But, no! A few yards away was an apple core which Gideon had left for the birds. It was time to return to the more mundane things of life, so, slowly I got up and walked back to the office.

CHAPTER
5

T he days rolled by slowly with summer blending into autumn. Those lovely, lazy, fall days where all you want to do is to sit under a tree and dream of far-off things, of distant shores and far horizons. I had not seen or heard from Gideon in days and wondered what had become of him.

Although he had made a strong impression on me, I preferred not to think about it. I was not unfamiliar with what he had said, since I had read books about such things. I even had some friends who were considered to be psychically gifted but still the effect Gideon had on me was different. He had spoken of the awesome potential of the human mind and of how we only used a small portion of it. He had pointed out that most people were content to be left in their misery and that these same people refused to see the very light that would change their misery to joy. I could almost hear his voice as he spoke to me that time in the park.

A close friend of the family would be visiting us soon. June Mareena Ridley was a most special friend. She was a clairvoyant, a person who could "see" events before they happened. At parties and get-togethers, she would do "mind stuff" that never ceased to amaze us.

I met her many years ago when I was completing a graduate business degree, part-time, at a major university. I had just finished my last class of the evening and was leaving when a poster on the bulletin board caught my attention. It stated that the internationally renowned psychic, June M. Ridley, would be giving a lecture and demonstration in the auditorium at 10:30 a.m. the following day.

Never having met a real psychic in my life, I thought that it would be interesting to see one. At that time, I was employed by a small manufacturing company and had responsibilities in the production area. Because I was new at the job, it would be difficult to leave during regular working hours to go to a lecture.

At work the next morning, however, a nagging, uneasy feeling came over me. I had a strong urge to attend the lecture. It was as if I were being pushed to go and listen to June. The more I tried to overcome the feeling, the stronger it became. Finally, I gave in to the compulsion. I gave a feeble excuse to my employer and drove as fast as I legally could to the university.

It was after 10:30 a.m. when I arrived and the lecture had already begun. I intensely dislike being late. Generally, I arrive for an appointment early and would rather wait in a parking lot or reception area than be even one minute late. This time, however, I could not help it. I rushed into the auditorium. Almost all the seats were occupied. In the front row, however, there was a lone, empty seat which I quickly took. It was so quiet in the room you could hear a pin drop.

Behind the podium was an attractive, middle-aged woman of medium height. She looked at me, smiled and continued the lecture. I felt that the audience seemed to be annoyed at my lateness and I thought to myself, angrily, "I want to be late, O.K.?" But after a few moments, the meaning of what the woman was saying caught up with me. She told us about her ability to "see" things before they occurred and how she was able to give what are called "readings" to people. She explained that she was born with the "gift of seeing," that each and every human being had the ability to develop those same talents. She spoke of God, angels and spirits, of different dimensions and different worlds. I was just beginning to think that I had wasted the entire morning when she decided to give us a demonstration of what she meant by the "gift of seeing."

She asked if anyone in the audience had ever seen or met her before in person. No one had. Beginning with the back of the room, she pointed to people at random and told them a little about themselves and their lives. To one especially nervous woman, she said, "Your friend Elizabeth will be getting married soon and will be moving out of the area. She is so concerned about her sick mother that she needs all the support you can give her. Do you understand what I mean?" The woman was simply astounded. "Yes! Yes! That is so true," she stammered.

After a few more "readings" she turned to a tall, dark man somewhere in the middle rows. "The trucking business which you are about to start will become a tremendous success," she said. "Watch out, however, for one of your partners—the short one, with the beard and funny hat. He will try to take control of the company away from you. Do you understand what I am talking about?"

"That's amazing," said the man, "Absolutely amazing. There was no way you could know about my trucking business," and he kept shaking his head in astonishment.

By this time, I was becoming very excited about the possibility of my turn. June pointed to a few others and told each of them something but totally ignored me. Perhaps she was doing this to me because I came in late, I thought paranoically, but I knew that couldn't be the reason.

Finally, because she had been speaking for

such a long time, she asked if someone could bring her a glass of water. Here was my opportunity to be noticed. Up I jumped and rushed to the water fountain in the hallway. Using one of the paper cups, I hurriedly brought June some water. Surely now she would notice me and tell me something about the future. I was wrong again. Not a word did she say to me.

As the lecture came to an end, I sat there, progressively more dejected. After she thanked everyone for coming, she looked at me and said, "Young man, I'll see you later. What I have to tell you would not be understood by anyone here, least of all by you." I was surprised but happy that she would at last tell me something about my future.

The professor who organized the lecture arranged for me to see June a short while later. It was one of the most amazing things that had ever happened to me. Without having seen me before or knowing anything about my past, she told me about my job, my family and where and how I lived. She said that in less than six months I would have new employment, but that I should not be concerned about it. It would be the birth of something new for me, but, she said, like all births, it would be painful for a short while. She continued for almost an hour telling me about my past, present and future and touched on things that only I knew. While she was speaking she seemed to be in another world. Her voice was soft, sweet and peaceful. The meeting ended.

Giving me her phone number, she said, "I would really like to meet you again. You and your wife should come visit soon." And so we did a few months later.

We soon became very good friends. Many of the things she had foretold began to take place. In less than six months I lost my job when the company moved to another state. Although I remained unemployed for a while before finding another position, I used the time to start my own small, part-time, janitorial business. Since then, many things changed for the better. The company grew and diversified. We moved from the apartment into a house and then a few years later into a much larger one.

Throughout the years, June remained a constant friend and advisor. Every six months or so, between her radio shows or television interviews, she would visit us for a week or two. These visits were very special times. By this time, my wife and I were the parents of two beautiful children and June would spend hours with them.

Little Malika was a favorite of June's and Jonathan would keep her busy for hours. So it was with joy and excitement that we were once again awaiting the arrival of June. We had not seen her in almost six months, so there would be much to talk about. We were now totally used to her strange abilities and hardly questioned them at all. We had certainly seen enough over the years to know that she had that rare "gift of seeing."

It had been one week since I last saw Gideon. With June's arrival, I'd almost completely forgotten about him. At the dinner table, June told us about her most recent television interview. It was always interesting listening to her describe such events. Although she would give readings to anyone, her clientele also included some of the rich and famous. Movie stars, politicians and high level business leaders consulted with her on a regular basis.

A short while later the children were tucked into bed and June, Mardai and I retired to the family room. Our house was built in the form of an "H" with the sleeping area occupying one section of it. The living rooms—there were two of them—were in the center of the "H" and the kitchen, dining room and family room were on the other side. Because the family room, being on the far side, was completely separated from the bedrooms, it was possible for us to talk and laugh to our hearts' content without disturbing the children who were sleeping peacefully.

On one side of the room was a fireplace and across from that was a piano, a gift from my wife's father. The piano bench was slightly pulled away from the piano. We had been talking for only a short while when June turned to me and said, "The man sitting on your piano bench says that he is here to help you in your understanding of new things." Having known June for such a

55

long time, we should have been used to such comments, especially when only the three of us were there and I was the only man present.

I looked across to the piano and saw only an empty bench. "What man are you speaking of, June?" I asked.

She said, "The one over there. He is now looking at you and smiling."

"Don't do that to us. You know that I can't see anyone sitting there."

"He says that you do know him, John, that you've met before. He has a beard and dark, piercing eyes. He says that he wishes to help you in your growth and learning and that you've been 'going through' experiences instead of 'growing through' them."

The description fit Gideon perfectly. "What's his name, June?"

"I can't get the exact sound but it seems to be Simeon . . . or no . . . it has a 'G'. It starts with a 'G'. His name is Gideon. He said that you ought to know the spelling because not too long ago you saw it on a license plate. He laughed as he said that. He said that you ought to keep an open mind. He is saying good-bye now and that he will see you again soon. Now he's gone."

So, it was Gideon again. But I could not see him this time. Neither could Mardai. Only June saw him. But then, she always saw things that others could not. We discussed this for a while and I recounted how it was that I met Gideon and the events that occurred thereafter. June seemed to understand and asked, like Gideon, that I keep an open mind.

"It is your strict scientific background that causes you to stumble many times, John."

She was right. I was always trying to be logical about everything. In my early days, I was trained as a chemist—labs, doing research and analyzing. Perhaps, more than many, I insisted on seeing before believing. And this, in spite of the fact that I knew June and her abilities.

The most successful times in my life were when I guided myself by the "still, small voice." Some people call it "gut feelings." The times that caused me the most problems were those where I drowned out the "voice" with logic and analysis. It was already three in the morning so we decided to turn in.

CHAPTER

Sunday morning, June left for home. We said our good-byes, promising to meet again soon. Her last words to me were, "Remember that the man who sat on the piano bench will be in touch with you, John. Listen to him and keep an open mind."

To clarify the many confused thoughts in my mind, I decided to go for a walk in the woods behind my house. I took Rajah with me. He likes nothing better than to run free in the woods. About three hundred yards from the house is a small open spot in the middle of the trees and bushes. In that clearing is a giant rock with many smaller rocks around it. Legend has it that centuries ago, a mysterious tribe of American Indians lived in the area. Perhaps, I thought,

61

this used to be a place of their high worship ceremonies. We walked into the clearing.

It was quiet and peaceful by the rock. The morning sun streamed through the leaves and branches of the tall trees to fall directly on the little patch where Rajah and I stood. The peace and quiet seemed to reach back in time; it felt like long, long ago in another country and another clime.

In my youth, it was a joy for me to spend hours in the forests. And forests and streams were plentiful. The little village where I was born could not have covered any more than two square miles. To the north of it was the Atlantic Ocean and to the south were all the tropical forests that a little boy could ever want. There was always the subtle call of the ocean, a sea song luring me to distant shores. The forests would also sing, but their songs reminded me more of the joys of existence where I was. It was a small fishing and farming village which was literally cut out of the jungle by my grandfather and a group of stalwart men.

Year after year the village grew as the inhabitants fought back the jungle and the sea. It always seemed that both wanted to reclaim the little village as a prize. In time, the village would become extremely prosperous, only to die years later when I was far, far away. It was my little village and thoughts of those times raced through my mind like birds on the wing.

"It is in remembering the times of your

strength and overcomings that you can grow stronger and overcome yet more." The voice interrupted my thoughts that roamed the little village streets of long ago. Looking around, I saw the speaker sitting on a rock next to mine. He was dressed like a story-book character, bright colors, funny hat and cowboy boots.

"Gideon! What are you doing here? Where did you come from?" The surprise in my voice startled Rajah.

"Just came from a party. Some folks in another time and another place."

"I am beginning to believe that you do the crazy things you talk about, like time travel and nonsense of that nature."

"You would do well to believe the things I tell you, John. Time travel is far from being nonsense. It is done regularly by those who know how. There are some of us who commute to other times just as simply and easily as you commute to other places."

"Were you in my house the other night?"

"Sitting on your piano bench. You couldn't see me, but your friend June saw me."

"Why couldn't I see you?"

"You were looking only with your physical eyes. Had you looked with your inner eye, you would have seen me too."

"Things like an inner eye and time travel seem so much like science fiction to me. Do you really think that people can travel through time? I mean. . . ."

He interrupted me. "You travel through time already. One method should be obvious to you. You were awake at six-thirty this morning and it's almost ten-thirty now. You have travelled almost four hours since you got up this morning."

"That's silly. Everyone does that."

"Because it is so obvious, no one ever observes the process carefully. It's taken for granted. It's called existing or living. The other method is more fun—or more frightening, depending on the encounters. You travel through time in your dreams. There it happens automatically. The conscious mind is removed from its monitoring functions. The other parts of you, which accept the seemingly miraculous as natural, function in their own time and space."

"But that happens without any rhyme or reason. Dream times are uncontrollable."

"Not quite, if you really understand how it works. What time does your watch read right now?"

"Ten-thirty on the dot."

"I will give you a demonstration. Think of a time way back in your past that you would like to see again if you could. Close your eyes and hold that thought in your mind for a few seconds."

I thought of an incident in college many years ago. A well-known speaker was giving a lecture and I had decided to get a cup of coffee at the cafeteria since I had enough time before the lecture started. I was enjoying my coffee at a table in the corner when a man walked up to me and asked, "May I join you?"

I replied, "Of course," and he sat down. Our conversation had lasted for about an hour. I wished I could go back to that scene for only a short while.

Gideon said, "Let's go and see your college incident again."

He had hardly said the words when there was a swirling sensation. When it stopped, I opened my eyes. Imagine my surprise to find myself and Gideon standing in the cafeteria of my old college. There were other students around and I began to worry about how I would explain our being there when Gideon said, "Don't worry. They can't see us or hear us. You're visiting another time. They will only be able to see us if we so desire. It's better this way at first."

He led me to a small table across from where we were standing. Two people were having coffee. Somehow, they seemed familiar to me.

"Do you know who those people are, John?" asked Gideon.

I looked a little closer and was shocked to see that the younger man was me—not me as I was today, but the me I was many years ago in college. There I was as a young college student sitting with another person, sipping coffee. "We are looking back in time, John," Gideon said. "That was the event you were thinking of when we left your present time situation. Look at the other man. Do you remember that he came up to your table, sat with you for a while and then went on to give his lecture?"

"That was Dr. Martin Luther King! I didn't know that when he first sat down, but by the end of our conversation, he told me who he was."

"Do you recall the effect of his conversation on you?"

"How could I ever forget? The kindness and the vision of that man! For years I will remember."

"You see, we can visit events of the past and observe them and you can remember them and learn from them."

I was fascinated. I stood there looking at them and listening to their conversation. Finally Gideon said, "It's time for us to leave here and go on to another time and place."

A thought struck me. "Could we have participated in their conversation, Gideon? I mean, the me of then and the me of now conversing with each other?"

"Yes! But there are certain rules one has to observe. For now, let's go."

The words were barely spoken when I felt the return of the swirling sensation. The entire scene changed and we were standing on the bank of a river. Coming towards us was a young man dressed in Hindu clothing. "You will notice, John, that we can participate in this event," said Gideon.

The man walked up to us, smiled at me and spoke to Gideon. "Hello! They told me that you

would be here soon, so I hurried to meet you."
Gideon seemed to know him and introduced me:
"My friend Krishna, of Hindu mythology."

The two of them kept up a lively conversation
as we walked to the water's edge. I stood on a
large flat rock and looked over the calm waters.
It was a beautiful morning with the sun shining
brightly.

"What river is this?" I asked Krishna.

"It is a tributary of the river Ganga—what you
would call the Ganges. It will, in time, become
the holiest of rivers for Hindus, just as the
Jordan will become the holiest of rivers for
Christians and Jews alike."

Krishna walked over to the rock on which I
was standing. He placed his foot on it and then
moved over a bit. As I looked down, I saw a
footprint where there was none before.

"Did you do that?" I asked.

He smiled mischievously. "They will speak
about it for generations to come. Yea! For thousands of their earth years, until they learn to
direct their footsteps towards the light which
beckons to all of us."

"Don't the Hindus speak of you as the most
important manifestation of their god Vishnu? I
mean, in the twentieth century, they actually
worship you and sing praises to you. How do you
feel about that?"

"We are all manifestations of God, but the sad
part of earth life is that whenever any one person
points the way to a better and more fulfilling life,

very quickly his followers forget the way and start worshipping the way-shower."

"It is an interesting thought," I replied for want of something more profound to say.

"Gideon is a close friend of mine," said Krishna. "We have known each other for eternity. He has agreed to work with you and teach you some of the eternal truths. Listen to him and you will find that you are listening to yourself. Life is a joyous adventure. Enjoy life."

A sudden peace came over me as I stood there on the banks of the most sacred of Hindu rivers. I felt at one with the world, at one with the universe. Perhaps, this was what was meant by "atonement," actually, "at-one-ment." Gideon said to me, "We must return now." We said good-bye to Krishna and then there was that swirling sensation again, and in the blink of an eye, we were back in the woods behind my house.

My watch read ten-thirty. Rajah was sitting exactly where we had left him, apparently totally unconcerned. Gideon was standing next to me. "Sit down," I said, motioning towards a large rock, "perhaps you could explain some of this to me."

I stretched out on the grass under the green trees and waited for Gideon to explain.

CHAPTER

Gideon settled himself on a rock and turned somewhat to make himself more comfortable. "Time is like the tides," he said, "or more properly, like a river. There are currents, white and dark water, backwash and so forth. Human beings, as they exist on earth, have been conditioned from birth to believe in sequential time, that is, time as moment after moment. By the ripe old age of five or six, one has generally forgotten the intricacies of the nature of time and space and thus is ready to live in a world where tomorrows come after todays and yesterdays lead to todays."

Much as one part of me wanted to understand what he was talking about, the other part of me was firmly anchored in the twentieth century.

"Stop, Gideon, I don't really think that all that is important. In fact, I am relatively comfortable in this time slot. What with television, computers, space shuttles and so forth, who knows? This could still be fun."

"If you don't blow yourself up first, or die of asphyxiation because there is no more breathable air. No water to drink eventually because your rivers and streams have been poisoned by chemicals."

"Oh it's not that bad. But let's get back to this 'time' thing. We did visit different times, didn't we?"

"Yes, indeed we did."

"Tell me about the classic case, Gideon. Suppose I had gone back to the time when my great-grandfather was a boy. Suppose we met, there was a fight and he was killed. Just suppose, O.K.? Would I be here now? Would I be there or anywhere? Explain that. How could I have been born if my great-grandfather had died as a boy? Ha! Got you on that one!"

"Pretty clever, but still at the kindergarten level. In that possible lifetime you would not have lived as such, but in another and another and a hundred thousand others you live and are as vibrant and alive as you are here."

"You mean that there are thousands of me living in thousands of different situations in thousands of worlds? Come on, Gideon."

"Let us not get too involved in this matter of 'time', John. It's rather an advanced concept.

72

Suffice it to say that, we, you, anyone with some practice could travel into different times and different places. Control your thoughts and you control your existence in space and time."

"That's fine for space and time but I am getting hungry. I can't take you home and introduce you to my family. What would I say? 'Here, meet my good friend Gideon who dresses funny, travels through time and knows Krishna'?"

"Your family would not be able to see me at this time. And as for being hungry, look at your watch. What time is it?"

I glanced at my watch and saw that it was still only ten-thirty, although we had been talking for what appeared to be hours, not counting the "trips" we had made. It seemed as if time hadn't passed. I looked at him and said, "You certainly couldn't stop time, could you? Not even *you* could do that."

"No. All we did was center ourselves in an area of non-movement of time and so it appears that time stood still. Not to worry though. All is well with you and your family and the world, if you will. No side effects."

I looked across to Rajah. He was sleeping peacefully. Next to him was a picnic basket. "What's that, Gideon?" I asked, pointing.

"Just lunch. You said you were hungry, didn't you? I brought it with me this morning. Let's have some."

Strange, but I hadn't noticed the basket before. We helped ourselves to a delicious lunch while Gideon continued his discourses on the universe.

"It's really simple," he said. "In fact, very simple when you understand it. Each person exists in many dimensions and many systems. Each one inhabits the entire universe, but most times is focussed in only one tiny spot—the here and now. But that is precisely the most important spot in life, the here and now. From that spot, each one influences his entire 'future' and 'past'."

"You know, Gideon, our church fathers would string you up for saying such things. What with all this nonsense talk about being born again, or having lived before? Surely, you don't believe that. . . ."

He interrupted me again. "You live as many lifetimes as are needful on earth. In each lifetime, you learn and strive to be better than the one 'before,' if you accept time as sequential. If you accept time as eternally now, then you exist in many systems and dimensions simultaneously."

It was a rather pleasant and 'learningful' morning. It was, however, time to get back to being normal and to see present time and people as I knew them.

"Don't be too hard on yourself, John. You have actually done well. I am, as you now can see, an other-worldly being. So are all of you on earth. You are just visitors here. Some of you know this. Others of you prefer to remain ignorant of that fact. Whichever way you prefer, you still have access to awesome power. See you soon."

And then he was gone. The lunch basket was also gone. Not even a leftover crumb. Only Rajah and I were there. I got up and walked back to the house.

CHAPTER

The remainder of Sunday was enjoyable. I have little trouble with week-ends. It is the time between week-ends that sometimes gives me problems. All too soon Monday arrived. The ride to the office was taken up with reflections of the past few days. June's visit had been most welcome, but too short. Yet, as always, we would be seeing her again, soon.

Gideon amazed and intrigued me. There was no doubt in my mind that he had access to considerable power. I accepted some of his concepts, such as time travel, as a distinct possibility, especially since I was a party to some of those journeys with Gideon. But it was again time to return to the tangible world of facts and "reality."

As usual, I was the first one to arrive at the office. I walked in and turned on the lights. He was sitting on one of the chairs across the desk from mine. "Gideon! Not you again!" I exclaimed.

"It seems as if you're getting bored with me, John," he said with a twinkle in his eye.

"No, of course not," I hastened to assure him, "Not bored, just puzzled that you always appear in the strangest places."

"That's good to know. I came because I felt that you were going to need to see a bit more clearly today." He did not smile this time and was more serious than I'd ever known him to be.

"What do you mean, Gideon?"

"You are afraid," he said, "for your employees, your family, your friends and others. You think that you have done all you could to make things better and yet you feel that you cannot see the light."

"You seem to be reading my mind again, Gideon. What you say is true, but I'm only human."

"Only human, John? Only human?" He was intense as he continued. "You use that as an excuse. You are much more than just human. You and all others are more divine than human. You were all created in the image and likeness of the First Force, the Almighty. Don't you remember the various legends of creation?"

"Yes, of course. So what? I am human or divine or both. It really doesn't matter. I'm still concerned about myself and my people and, because of my concern, I sometimes fear and tremble. Is it so terrible to care for others? Is it a sign of weakness to be concerned about your fellow human beings? What's so terrible about that?"

"No, not the caring, John. The worrying is what gets you. You must make a distinction between caring and worrying. You care, so you try to make everything work right. When nothing seems to work right, you worry and become fearful and because of the fear, you short-circuit yourself."

"In what way or manner, O Great One?" I asked somewhat sarcastically.

"You see, John, the rules are really very simple. The Creator made everything and all of us. We also are creators. We are endowed with many of the qualities of the Creator, but most times, these qualities are so deeply buried that they're hardly ever recognized or used."

"Yes, Lord and Master, please continue for your humble servant."

He ignored my attitude and continued. "Worry is a form of directed energy, John. Worry removes your focus from everything else and directs it in a concentrated manner on that which you fear. Worry and fear then join to bring into your existence the very thing of which you were afraid."

"So, how do I stop worrying? Tell me that."

"You stop worrying when you understand the

81

universal laws that make things work. One of those laws says that whatever you see in your mind—good or bad—if you believe it, it will come to pass. Creation starts in your mind with your thoughts and imagination. Cause and effect world, John. Use insight and you will see right. What you sow, you shall reap. As you think and believe, so it becomes."

"Good sayings, Gideon. I know most of those things but how do I use that knowledge in a practical way? How do I use it to better the situation in which I find myself right now?"

"By centering yourself and looking within you. This is an inside job, you see. The answers are all within you. Not outside, not in someone else and not even in the one you call God."

That puzzled me for a second. "I thought that God could do everything. Why wouldn't He have the answers? Why, more importantly, wouldn't He give us some of those answers especially when we pray to Him so earnestly?"

"Because you don't understand God and the methods He gave us for finding answers. We don't have to beg or plead. We only have to relax and become quiet and to believe in ourselves and the abilities inherent in us. Then we'd begin to get answers in the form of ideas. We must believe and trust the process. God doesn't withhold our good from us. Often we're just unable to see that we already have—or can have—what we want."

This discussion set me to thinking about God.

Humankind seemed to have so many gods. The Muslims had one, the Christians another, the Jews yet another and others even more and different gods. Some had more than one. Various religions located their "gods" in places such as temples, mountains, streams and skies. Legends spoke of greater and lesser "gods."

Even I had a god with whom I was vaguely acquainted. I had learned in Sunday school that He lived in a place called heaven. He seemed so far removed from everyone and everything that only popes and priests, pastors and preachers, kings, emperors and presidents had access to Him. One would lift beseeching hands and cry in pain to this "god" but most times, no answer. I thought I'd throw a curve at Gideon.

"Hey, Gideon, you know so much. Tell me about God. Who and what is He? Why doesn't He hear when people cry to Him? Tell me if you can."

Without blinking an eye, Gideon answered, "Your religions are like schools in different countries. They teach you basically the same thing but in different languages and in different ways. Some schools may stress art or history, while others may place more emphasis on chemistry or math. But there is a common thread in all of them—they lead to the same place, the Temple of Wisdom and Light. So God by any other name is still God. The cry of the ancient Hebrews, 'Hear, O Israel, the Lord thy God is One,' is as true now as it was then, or ever will be.

"God is not in a place or time. God is here and now. Heaven or hell is here and now. God does not sit on a golden throne surrounded by angels who play harps or fly all day. If you think that is what heaven is, you had better start taking flying lessons or learn to play the harp. God is in each person, in each life form, in each and every part of creation. God is no more or less present in you than in another life form at the edge of the galaxy.

"And God listens and cares. He is concerned even about sparrows and lilies of the field. Would He not be concerned about you, or for that matter, me?"

I was sorry I brought it up. We could talk about that for days. Again I changed the direction of the conversation. Gideon never seemed to mind my doing that. "Why don't I see clearly what must be done for this company I am trying to build? Is it necessary that all this, which took a lifetime to build, be torn apart or destroyed?"

Patiently, Gideon responded, "If it has to be that way for your greater good, then accept it. If it doesn't have to be that way, then that is also fine. But you're the one who has to decide. Prepare yourself for that which you are seeking. Know that what you are seeking is also seeking you. You want a successful corporation? Then prepare for it. Know that the forces of the universe will rush in to bring that which you want, provided of course, you want it badly

84

enough and believe that you can get it. Or better yet, deserve it.

"All problems on earth are of three types. They are health, money and relationships. Name any problem and it will fall under one of these three categories or a combination of two or more of them. There are proper and correct methods to solve a problem just as there are to drive a car or to build a house.

"Now, I must leave you again, John. There are many more things to discuss but we'll meet again soon. Incidentally, I would like to introduce you to a good friend of mine who may prove to be of some assistance to you. He has an office in the Big City. When you have a slow day, we could visit him. Would you like to do that?"

"Certainly. If he could help us with this financial thing, I would go to the ends of the world to meet him." Mischievously I added, "even if he's half as strange as you, it would be fun."

"I'm sure you'll like him. Let's go soon," he said. He stood up and smiled. "Have a good day, John." Then he was gone. It would be weeks before I would see him again.

CHAPTER

It was true that our company had finally managed to acquire a large contract but things still were not going the way we would have liked. Everyone was working very hard, but the results were not comparable to the efforts. Additional financing was urgently needed. Without such funds, the company would be unable to increase production to meet the necessary requirements of the contract. There was even the possibility of having to dissolve the corporation, but I didn't like to think about that.

At our last meeting, Gideon had mentioned that he wanted me to meet with one of his friends in the Big City. I was even more interested in the meeting now, if there was a possibility that it could lead me to the proper contacts for a business loan. Even if nothing came of it, at least I wouldn't have left any stone unturned. It could even turn out that the meeting would be fun, and there were such few "fun" things that I did these days. I thought I would call Gideon and see if I could make arrangements to go with him in the morning.

As I searched on my desk for his business card, the phone rang. It was, of course, he. "I see you're ready to go to the Big City," he said. "I'll meet you in your parking lot at nine-thirty tomorrow morning." Without waiting for an answer, he hung up.

At nine-thirty the next morning, I was in the parking lot and walking towards my car when I saw him. He was sitting, as pretty as you please, in my car waiting for me. Nothing surprised me about this man anymore. "Good morning, Gideon. Let's go," I said.

"I'm sure you'll have a fine morning, John," he replied.

As we drove out of the parking lot, I jokingly asked, "Why do we have to use a car, Gideon? I mean, you're able to traverse space and time. Let's do it the easy way. Let's arrive in the Big City instantaneously and avoid the traffic."

Those dark piercing eyes were distant as he answered. "I'll tell you a story," he said.

"Once upon a time in the ancient land of Bharat, there lived a Guru and his bramcharyas or as you would call them, disciples. Each disciple was supposed to pick as his test a very difficult task to do. He was to work exceedingly hard for several years to perfect himself in the task that he, himself, had set. There was this one disciple, somewhat brighter than the others, yet so very shy and timid.

"'And what task have you set for yourself, my son?' asked the kindly Guru.

"'Master,' answered the disciple, 'I want to be able to walk on water. I will practice until I'm able to do it. To walk on water, that is my goal.'

"Years passed and under the gentle guidance of the Guru, most of the disciples accomplished what they had set out to do. Finally, the shy disciple approached the Guru. 'Master,' said he, 'I have toiled and practiced without ceasing, lo, these many years. See that city across the river? I can now walk on the water and go over to the city. Master, I have overcome. I can walk on water.'

"The old master looked at the young one and sadly asked, 'Why did you not take the boat?'

"John, when you can walk on water, you generally take the boat."

I mumbled an "Oh," not quite getting the entire point of the story, but I didn't ask for an explanation. I don't always like to listen to riddles or parables and Gideon certainly had many of them. I prefer plain talk. I asked about the people we would be meeting today.

"I made all the necessary arrangements," he said. "You're expected."

"Are they business associates of yours?"

"Business associates and friends also."

"Do you think that I'll be able to get some assistance for the company?"

"A definite possibility," he replied.

"You know that we need a loan to continue our operations. Would they be willing to help us out in this situation?"

"Perhaps."

His short answers were beginning to annoy me. He seemed to be in a pensive mood this morning. Not wanting to appear rude, I gave up trying to make conversation. I was thinking only of myself and my problems forgetting that he too, could be occupied with his own problems. But then again, he shouldn't have any problems, not with the type of power he seemed to possess.

He broke into my thoughts saying, "Even God has problems. It's the way one goes about solving them that's interesting."

"God shouldn't have problems, Gideon. I mean, it doesn't make sense. God can do anything."

"True, but even God doesn't like boredom. To exist without challenges would be boredom at its ultimate."

He became quiet again, so I left him to his thoughts for a while. The drive was not too unpleasant. Usually, I don't like to drive to the Big City. Being there is one thing, but trying to get there is another. There are few things more unpleasant than being stuck in traffic for hours.

A flock of gulls had been flying above and to

the front of the car since we left the parking lot. To occupy time, I counted them. There were seven. The freedom of flight, I thought. Gideon broke the silence. "A flock of gulls by day and a pillar of fire by night," he said.

"What?"

"The ancient Israelites, you know, were led in their wanderings in the wilderness by a cloud by day and a pillar of fire by night."

"Three cheers for the Israelites," I mumbled, having no idea of what he was speaking.

In a short while, we arrived in the Big City. It was, as always, impersonal. We parked the car, paid the necessary fee and walked through the eternal crowds to a waiting cab. Gideon gave the driver an address and a few minutes later we stepped out in front of a tall building on a side street. We walked up to the door, entered and located the elevators. Gideon pushed a button and we were soon on our way to the thirty-third floor.

We stepped out into a long hallway. I took a few seconds to straighten my tie and comb my hair. The winds of the Big City could be exceedingly fierce at times. At the end of the hallway was a large door with a sign on it that read: "G & M Enterprises, Inc.—World Headquarters."

"These are the people with whom you work, right, Gideon?"

He was a little more relaxed now. "Yes," he said. "It's about time you got to meet my employer. There will also be another friend of mine here. You remember Marla?"

"Marla will be here, too? Oh yes, I forgot that she also works for this company. It'll be good to see her again."

There was that twinkle in his eye and I knew that he was back to his old self again. He pushed open the door and we walked into a reception area that was both simple and beautifully decorated at the same time. There were paintings on the walls with strange symbols on them. A receptionist looked up and smiled. "Hello, Gideon, and welcome to our office, John," she said.

"You look well, Mary," replied Gideon.

"Won't you sit down, please. Marla is here already. It will only be a few minutes," said Mary.

In a short while Marla joined us and we renewed old acquaintances. She seemed pleased to see me there. The receptionist left for a few moments and when she returned, she announced, "The chief will see you now."

She escorted us through the main area to an office with a sign on the door that read: "President and Chairman of the Board."

"Gee, Gideon, you know the boss," I teased.

As the door opened he said, "You'll enjoy this meeting, John."

We stepped into an office with thick carpeting of celestial blue. There were many well-kept plants properly placed throughout the well-lit room. On the far side was a large desk, behind which sat a rather imposing figure. We walked over to him and Gideon proceeded with the introductions.

"John, I'm pleased to introduce you to our chief executive officer. He is president and chairman of the board of G & M Enterprises." I noticed a great respect but no fear in Gideon's voice as he continued, "I want you to meet God."

For a moment I was shocked. Then I remembered that many people refer to their bosses as "god," and so, I was at ease once again. I looked over to the person behind the desk. He seemed to be middle-aged, possessing a powerful presence about him. His hair was jet black and his eyes dark and piercing, somewhat like Gideon's. Yet as I looked at him a little more carefully, his hair now appeared to be lighter and his eyes blue. Must be some trick of the light, I thought.

He got up from his chair, shook my hand and said, "Glad you could come. My thanks to Marla and Gideon for getting you here. I've been waiting for your visit for a long time."

I mumbled something to the effect that it was also good to be here and that I had been looking forward to this meeting. The one known as "God" was informally dressed—not even a tie—although his shirt appeared to be expertly tailored and there was an unrecognizable insignia over the right pocket. He motioned to us to sit and asked whether we would care for something to drink. None of us wanted anything so I sat waiting anxiously for someone to start the conversation.

Gideon was the first to speak. "John, you don't seem to understand. This isn't a joke. You're in the presence of God. I mean, *the* God with a capital 'G'." I started feeling uneasy again. It was impossible for someone to be speaking face-to-face with God. They did that in movies and books, but not in real life. Reason dictated that this was all nonsense, yet there was a part of me that said it was all right for me to believe, at least for the time being, that there was more to this than met the eye. My curiosity prevailed and I decided to accept all this for a while and see where it would take me.

God spoke this time. The voice was neither too high nor too low and resounded with a vibrant life force. "John," He said, "Even now, you still don't believe that I am who they say I am, right?"

"Well, it's hard to do so," I replied.

"I understand. However, make yourself comfortable because we'll be here for a while. Excuse me. I'll be back in a few seconds." With that he got up and left the room.

CHAPTER
10

Marla and Gideon just sat there staring at me when the door closed. Finally Marla asked, "Well, what do you think, John?"

"Think? What do I think? This is perhaps the most amazing thing that has occurred to me in ages and you're asking me what I think? It's difficult for me to think at all."

"Accept this with an open mind," said Gideon, "and you will find that there are different ways to approach life."

The door opened and God returned. There was a tremendous sense of peace and joy when he was near and yet I still could not consciously bring myself to believe that this was *the* God. He walked over to his chair and sat down. Looking me straight in the eye, he said, "John, you don't really believe all of this, do you?" It was more a statement than a question.

"Well, I must admit that I am puzzled."

"I *am* God. I am Alpha and Omega, the beginning and the end, First Cause, Jehovah, Yahweh, Yeshua, Allah. I am I—Lord God Almighty—The First Force. What did you expect to see? What do you think God should look like? An old man sitting on a throne? Dozens of angels dancing around him, her or it? God *is* God and *is* all things to all people."

He gave the appearance of a man totally in control of himself. His voice and tone were not in the least reprimanding, but rather, understanding and kind. I did not know what to say so I blurted out the first thing that came to mind. "How come," I asked, "I am here with you, when there are many others more deserving of an audience with you than I am?"

"That is one of the problems," he said. "Almost everyone thinks that I am unreachable, that I only speak to special people in special places and at special times. Listen carefully: Everyone is special to me. I speak to everyone but not all listen. I appear to everyone in many ways, but not all see. Do you remember that little child to whom you gave some money the other day? That was me speaking to your heart and feelings. Do you remember the time that you stopped and helped an old man fix a flat tire on the bridge that leads to the Big City? That was me again."

"You mean that you care about little things like flat tires?"

"Of course I care. And there are no little things, only people who tend to look at things and call them little. Take a rose, for example." As he said that, a beautiful rose appeared, as if by magic, in his hand. "Consider the intricacies of it. Surely, not a little thing. I love roses. They brighten everyone's life. In fact, I love everything that I've created."

"Well, if you are God, why do you have an office in the Big City? How is it that you are president and chairman of the Board of G & M Enterprises anyway?"

"G & M stands for God and Man. It's my 'earth' company. What better place to have an office than in the Big City? We have branches in almost every city on earth. In every town and little village you can find us. We also have a number of subsidiaries. Marla and Gideon are from the corporate office. Marla is in P. R.—'people recycling' in this case and Gideon is a trouble-shooter, special projects. You're one of his projects."

"It sounds so business-like, as if the entire world were a giant corporation."

"I compare it to a business for your understanding. You understand the corporate world, so I speak to you in terms of what you understand. You see, I'm in business—the 'God Business'—or, looking at it another way, the 'Good Business'."

101

If this were God, I thought, then I would be privy to a rare privilege indeed and should take full advantage of it. Actually, I was beginning to take him seriously.

His voice broke into my thoughts. "You need proof that I am God. Yet, no matter what proof you're given, you'll always find that there is an element of doubt. That doubt as to whether you did the right thing, is a result of your having the power of choice. Let me tell you this. After I had made the earth and all that was in and on it, I too, wondered whether it was the right thing. But, then again, whatever I do *is* the right thing."

"Did Gideon get his powers from you?"

"Yes, and so did you. Now, let me show you something. Think of a place where you would like to be."

"How about the Serengeti plains of East Africa?"

"Good. You will see. . . ." and before the sentence was finished, I found myself on a grassy plain with shrubbery dotting the landscape. There were the acacia trees of tropical Africa. Wildebeests, giraffes and elephants were all around. The transition was so instantaneous that I caught my breath. But, then again, didn't Gideon take me to other places and times? Surely, the one who called himself God could do the same.

Suddenly, there was a movement in the tall grass to my right. My previous trips to the

Serengeti plains had been taken using more conventional fare such as airplanes, enclosed jeeps and native guides. This time, I was all alone except for the animals around me. Then there was a sound. A chill went down my spine. I turned around to find facing me, not more than thirty paces away, the largest black-maned lion I had ever seen.

It stared at me with fiery eyes that froze the very marrow in my bones. He crouched, ready to spring, and I knew without a doubt that such a situation was not conducive to longevity. I couldn't move. I just stood there, rooted to the ground. With an earth-shattering roar, the lion sprang. I felt the hot breath of the carnivore just inches away. My arms were raised instinctively. Then a blur, and I was back in the office with Marla, Gideon and God.

"Don't be afraid," said God, "you're not in any danger. Enough of this."

Although still shaken from my experience, I continued to look at him. All of sudden, it seemed as if I were looking through different eyes than mine, as if a new world were opening before me. I felt the presence of an extremely powerful force. And then, as if by a miracle, I felt I was looking at the face of God. I fell to my knees in awe and whispered, "Forgive me, Lord. Although I didn't believe at first, now I know that You are truly my Lord and my God."

"Get up," He said, with warmth and love in His voice, "No need to fall on knees and stuff like that." I got off my knees and sat down as God continued to speak. "It is easy to set up barriers and to keep those barriers for a lifetime. You have all built walls, not only nation against nation, but neighbor against neighbor, friend against friend. You've even built such walls between yourselves and me. In your present state, you've forgotten the joy and bliss of being close to me, yet, if you search your deepest memories you may have a vague recollection of what it was like when the sons and daughters of God danced with joy on the 'morning' of creation.

"This isn't the only place where life forms exist. Look up into the sky some clear night and see the millions of stars—universes within universes. Look up and you will know that you're not alone in that vast expanse you call space. There are others, many others and all of them are my children."

While God spoke, I had no desire to go anyplace or do anything. I felt such a peace and happiness that I forgot about my corporation and its financial troubles. Nothing seemed important except to sit there and be with Him and listen.

God continued, "The universe is dynamic and changing. It continues to grow. Creation never stopped. It will continue forever. Wherever you are is the center of the universe and the midpoint of infinity. Nothing is static. All things change. But I do not change. The part of you that is Me and the part of Me that is you will forever remain changeless. So even though seasons change and worlds change, I, God, do not change."

"Lord, I'm overwhelmed," I said.

"You can interrupt me at anytime and ask questions. Don't be afraid to speak. Because I am God, I don't become offended or feel insulted. I wish my children would interrupt me more often. Now as I was saying, in this world of change, you have chosen to be here. . . ."

"Chosen to be here, Lord? How could we possibly have 'chosen' to be born?"

"Do you think for one instant that you appeared out of nothingness into the body you currently have? No, you existed before and will continue to exist after your body is gone. And as to the choosing process. . . ."

I interrupted Him again. "Pardon me, but are you saying that we were living, thinking beings before we were born? And that we chose to be here? I mean, how come we don't remember?"

"First," God answered, "if you insist on the framework of 'time' as you understand it—in a before and after continuum—yes, you were conscious energy beings before this earth life.

"Because of the challenges and opportunities for growth and experimentation in an earth life, many of you chose to come here. You chose the country, the period of history, your parents and even your friends. You made an agreement prior to your earth birth. The agreement took place at levels that you don't consciously remember.

But the higher self of you, that self which knows me well, understands and remembers.

"If your conscious self would listen to your higher, inner self, you'd have the answers to many of your problems. You'd be guided in times of stress and comforted in times of sorrow. It is I who speak to you with the still small voice. Even in your loneliest moments, you are never alone. Even in the depths of the furnace of affliction, I'm there."

"Lord, I have a million questions," I said. "I don't know where to start."

"Why don't we continue our conversation in a place you'd really enjoy? Would you like to go on a short trip with Me, Gideon and Marla? I think you'll enjoy it."

"Certainly," I said, "Wherever You go, I want to be there."

God looked at Gideon and Marla and nodded. Immediately there was a shimmering and the surroundings disappeared.

CHAPTER
11

CHAPTER

11

The shimmering stopped and I looked around. We were on a large ship with no sight of land. As far as the eye could see there was water, blue and beautiful. The wind and waves were calm. Next to me stood Gideon, Marla and God. God smiled at me and said, "I thought a change of scenery would do you good, especially since you love the ocean so much."

The vessel was a tall ship replete with sails and rigging. There didn't seem to be anyone else aboard and I wondered who was sailing it. "Where are the sailors, Lord? Such a large ship must surely need sailors."

"Not this time, John," He said, "For navigation we're using a form of energy called 'celestial power.' It'll be a few more centuries before your scientists discover its existence."

We pulled up a few deck chairs and sat with our faces to the wind. It was a delightful setting, to say the least. How quickly one gets used to miracles.

"There aren't any miracles, John." It was God speaking. "If you understand universal laws, you would understand so-called 'miracles.' Everything works according to universal laws. Know the laws and your knowledge becomes power. Yet, even power needs the use of wisdom."

Next to us on a small table was a basket of fruit. There was also a jug with what appeared to be either water or juice. Gideon reached over and poured himself a glass. "Try some, John, it's good," he said. He poured me a glass of the most delicious fruit juice I had ever tasted. Marla took a banana instead. I looked at God to see what He would do. Surely, He did not eat or have a need to. God picked up a plum and bit into it.

He looked at me, winked and said, "I don't have to eat, John. In the cosmic sense, neither do you. But it's enjoyable, at least most times, if done properly and in moderation."

I couldn't quite understand what He meant by not having to eat.

He continued, "You see, on earth you have a physical body made of elements that are a part of the very earth itself. Your body is a marvel of engineering. I designed it to be relatively self-sustaining and self-correcting.

"If treated with respect and love, the body generally takes care of itself. It is, so to say, your house here on earth. Each of your cells is a unit of consciousness. They perform in concert to produce a symphony of higher complex vibrations. These vibrations affect every other cell in the entire body. These cells know exactly what's necessary for the body to exist in harmony with its environment. I placed the necessary engineering and electronic data in their memory. If given half a chance, they would keep you healthy. You think they're simple because you study them under your microscopes, but your most advanced computers are like stone age artifacts when compared to the intricacies of the life force in your cells.

"It's true that you need a certain amount of nutrients for your physical body, but that amount is usually small. Your mental body is woven into your physical body, yet, you feed one and not the other. Your concern for food for the physical far outweighs your concern for food for the mental and the spiritual. Listen, it is in the realm of mind that you control all in the physical. It is by working within that you change without. The problems appear on the outside, the solutions are on the inside."

"How then do you explain disease and illness? Shouldn't the body take care of these things?" I asked.

"Yes, there are diseases in your world, but they generally result from a condition called 'disease'. There are illnesses that humankind creates all the time. All diseases have their roots in your mind and beliefs. And the cure for all of them is already inherent in you. Most times, a fear of disease, deep in your subconscious, makes it possible for the disease to become a part of you. Think healthy thoughts and discount the possibility of disease and it will never come to live in your house.

"There are materials given to you to assist in keeping the body and mind 'healthy.' These are all around you but usually you ignore them and look for other ways. Take light and sound, for example. Your scientists are like children where the knowledge of light and sound is concerned. Only now, in your time, are they beginning to take a hard look at various intriguing possibilities. Vibrations of various kinds affect both the physical and mental bodies. Certain gems, colors and sounds are much more beneficial than others. You can generally tell in periods of deep meditation which ones would be best for you. If you cannot, you may need the help of a teacher or a practitioner in these matters. If your mind is calm and your outlook positive, you would naturally be drawn to the right people, the right place and the right things. You would feel that certain colors are good for you. You would feel the effects of certain sounds and light. Tune in to yourself and trust your guidance.

"You will be healthy, not by disliking sickness, but by loving health. Treat your body with respect and love. It is the vehicle for your consciousness while you are on earth. It's also made to provide you with pleasure. Looking at a beautiful sunset, tasting a delicious meal, hearing musical sounds, touching and so forth, these can be very pleasurable sensations for your body. You built it. I only designed it and provided the blueprint."

God stopped talking for a moment and took another bite of the plum. "Plums are good," He said. "Fruits and vegetables are good. There are herbs that are beneficial for specific bodily ailments. You can find out about these herbs by reading or by asking those who are knowledgeable. The ancients of your earth knew much about these things. There's much to be learned from what was handed down to you. But in the twentieth century, there's not much respect for knowledge of old. Your scientists have educated themselves to such an extent that often the very education itself has blinded many of them."

My thoughts were racing. This was extremely beneficial information. Marla added, "Take for example, John, the situation of weight control. Whenever you are heavier than you should be, a mental process could be used to adjust the weight. All you do is see yourself, in your mind's eye, having exactly the weight you desire. You must believe and know that the method will work. If this is done correctly, then within a short period that may last from a few days to a few weeks, your weight can adjust itself."

It was time, I thought, to ask a few questions concerning my current problems. Yet, such problems seemed so far away and not at all important today. There was no desire to even think of the everyday, mundane situations. Just being in the presence of the Almighty gave me a different perspective. But, nevertheless, I found myself asking, "Why is it, Lord, that sometimes when we work so hard toward a goal, it begins to seem ever further from us? In fact, there are so many things that I am working on and they all seem to get worse. Any light that You can shed will be a tremendous help, not only to me, but also to those I want to help."

"There are various reasons," said God. "The things for which you are striving so hard may not be things that you really want or need. Another reason may be that you aren't ready or prepared yet to handle those things. Or, it could be timing. You have to learn how to read the signs of the times. A good farmer knows when to sow and when to reap. He doesn't reap when he should be sowing or sow when he should be reaping."

Those reasons seemed too ordinary to be "God Answers," so I pursued the question. "I thought any time was a good or proper time. How do we know this timing? How can we find the right time?"

"It is true," replied God, "that anytime is a good time, but you must know if it is the *right* time. Winter is a good time, but do you plant roses in the snow? A stormy day is a good day, but is it a day for sailing or fishing? There are cycles in the universe, the world and your life. Learn to find the cycles and use them for your benefit. Things started at one time will be much more successful than if started at another time."

"Sounds something like astrology. Is there anything to that stuff?"

"I love puzzles, crosswords and other kinds. You have many puzzles in your lives. Things would be dull indeed without challenges. But, although the puzzles are challenging, you've been given clues. You have guidance systems for your earthly life. The sailors of old used the stars for navigation on the high seas. You too, could use the stars for navigation on the sea of life. How do you think those three wise men from the East found our little baby Jesus? Don't you remember the story? They studied the heavens. They saw a star and they were able to interpret the signs correctly. You may call it astrology, celestial navigation or whatever you please."

"Can the ordinary person use these things for his own guidance?" I asked.

"Even today," He said, "there are many who guide their paths according to the signs they read. These signs—astrological or otherwise—were not given to you as crutches, but as guideposts. They don't determine or predestine what will happen to you. *You* do that. They only point the way. *You* have to do the travelling.

"Most of my animals are more aware of cycles and signs than are human beings. Notice how they seem to know of approaching storms or earthquakes. They don't block out the messages they receive. But you, the epitomy of my creation on earth, have filled yourselves with so much worry and fear that you can't hear yourselves think. You can't even hear me speak to you. You refuse to look at the signs I've given you.

"Yet, those signs are there for anyone. In your sleep time you have signs and guidance through your dreams. In your waking time, there are just as many helpful signs for your direction and well-being. Take for example, reading license plates on cars. Every once in a while, take the letters you see and form words. Pick the first words that come into your mind and see how often those words have relevance to your present situation. Look at a billboard once in a while. Or perhaps a song on your favorite radio station gives you a hint. Open a book, any book, to any page and see what it tells you. There are 'sermons in stones' if you would but take the time to look, listen and be receptive."

A slight breeze arose and the sails billowed. The sound of the creaking masts joined with the ocean to create a beautiful windsong. I still had no desire to go anywhere or do anything, but just to sit there forever and ever and hear God speak. There was a faint, glowing light around Him. I had seen such a light before around Gideon, but this was the first time I saw it around Marla, also.

116

God continued. "Don't think that you always have to speak to me about sacred, holy or spiritual things. I enjoy many things, even a cruise, as you can see. Don't be afraid to confide in me. I'm closer to you than the air you breathe."

I thought that I would ask one question about my future, since I could sense that our meeting was fast coming to an end. "Lord," I asked, "will my pathway over the next months be a little easier than it has been?"

"The way you have chosen for yourself will be a difficult but glorious one. You'll need all the strength and faith you can muster for what lies ahead. But you *will* come through it. For me to tell you more would deter you from the path that you have set for yourself. As you go through the months ahead, remember that you are never alone. Reach out and hold my hand sometimes. You'll be amazed at how much it helps. Wherever you are, I am there with you."

There was a sweet sadness about all this. Gideon looked at me and said, "It's time to go back, John."

"Do I have to?" I asked.

It was God who answered. "Yes, John, but remember what you learned here today. You'll need it." Turning to Gideon and Marla, He said, "No need for John to worry about traffic today. Please make sure that he's back at his office without any problems." He looked at me again and as He said, "Go in peace," I felt as if I had always known Him.

117

The scene started to disappear. There was a brief silence and then Gideon and I were sitting in my car in the parking lot behind my office. Marla was nowhere to be seen. Gideon broke the silence. "The Lord moves in mysterious ways," he said, and then, he too was gone. I sat there for a little while longer, then slowly got out and walked to my office.

CHAPTER
12

The threads of history weave strange patterns in the webs of time. Mysterious and confusing as the weaving sometimes appears to be, the finished product is usually a thing of beauty. Often, one does not see the entire picture from the vantage point of only a portion of a lifetime. It is by expanding the mind and trusting the universal flow that it is possible to make sense of what may be considered nonsense or non-sense.

It was sometime in the late sixteenth or early seventeenth century. Far across the seas in the ancient land of Bharat, which today is known as India, mighty forces were at work. Somewhere in the north central part of that land, in an area inhabited by the descendents of fierce Rajput warriors, the Maharajah Jai Singh the Second had already made tremendous scientific advancements in the pink and lavender city of Jaipur.

A little boy about the age of ten served at the court of the powerful Jai Singh. This little boy's name, taken from another powerful ruler of earlier days, was Mahn Singh. Well versed was he with the stories told at court. On many an evening he would listen in quiet amazement as visitors from faraway places exchanged stories and tales with one another. As Mahn Singh grew older, he would dream of those distant lands across the seas. As he grew into manhood, he would tell and retell the stories he used to hear at court.

Thousands of miles across the oceans, England had a new queen. Elizabeth the First, daughter of Henry the Eighth, was a shrewd and powerful monarch. She was constantly at war with Spain, which was then ruled by Phillip the Second. In an all out effort to subjugate England, Phillip the Second dispatched what has been recorded in history as the Spanish Armada. The defeat of the Armada did not prevent the Spanish from trying to colonize parts of South America and the islands of the Caribbean.

On one of the Spanish expeditions led by Don Pedro da Silva, a young sailor by the name of Juan Martinez was watching an approaching storm. Great was the fury of that storm and when it abated, the entire crew, but one, was no more. All but Juan Martinez perished. He only survived by holding on to a piece of wreckage which he found floating near to him. Days passed under the hot, tropic sun until, finally, delirious and dehydrated, he was found by a strange band of warriors. He had drifted into the estuary of that mysterious South American river called the Orinoco.

It is said that Juan Martinez was taken to a city called Manoa, which was ruled by a legendary figure known as El Dorado—The Golden One. Beautiful indeed was the city. The streets were paved with gold and the houses and temples gloriously reflected the rays of the morning sun. Juan Martinez lived for many years among the natives of this land and then escaped one day to tell his story.

One who heard the story of El Dorado was Sir Walter Raleigh, friend and confidant of Elizabeth the First of England. Many expeditions were made to the area on the northern coast of South America called Guyana. It was there that Raleigh and others believed that the fabled golden city would be found.

In the search for El Dorado, many lives were lost. In the dense jungles of Guyana could be found bushes of Yellow Allamanda and Red Amaryllis. There was also the waxen petalled Cereus that blooms at midnight once in seven years, then fades away with the rising sun. But a land of wealth and ease or a golden city could not be found. Throughout the centuries, the fight for Guyana continued until, in the end, the country became a part of the British Empire.

In the meantime, the little boy Mahn Singh, who you may recall had spent much time at the court of the Maharajah Jai Singh the Second, had become an old man. His last days were spent much like his earlier days, telling stories of distant lands to his grandchildren and great-grandchildren. One great-grandson especially delighted in asking questions of the elderly Mahn Singh. Though still young in age, Jung Bahadur Singh would question Mahn Singh for hours about foreign lands and different peoples. He also learned about the heroes of the Ramayana as well as about the countries of the West where many adventures awaited the brave and restless ones who would dare journey beyond the land of their birth.

Jung Bahadur Singh was in his twenties when he heard of some of his people travelling across the ocean to work on the sugar plantations in a remote, tropical land called Guyana. Jung Bahadur Singh, great-grandson of Mahn Singh, took up the call and together with several other stalwart young men, shipped off to the only British colony on the mainland of South America.

If the conditions in India were difficult, the ones in Guyana seemed almost impossible. From early morn to late at night, Jung Bahadur Singh worked in the fields. He raised his family as best he could. Battling the encroaching jungles on one hand and the restless sea on the other so as to save his little farm, he persisted and struggled until the day he died. But the son of Jung

Bahadur Singh grew up in the little village by the ocean and remembered the tales of the land from which his father came.

The little village grew and prospered and in time, the son of Jung Bahadur Singh, whose name was Harricharan Nian Singh, planted his own crops and tended his own sheep and cattle. The tides of time rolled on, as always, and then a son was born to him. Nian Singh spent much time with his son, who later, in a radical departure from Hindu tradition, would be called John. He taught him the ways of the West and the wisdom of the East, believing that a blend of both would be better than either one alone. Nian Singh worked like his forefathers before him, in the fields and farms, so that he could afford to educate his son in the better schools of that time. Much was learned by John and then one day, like his grandfather, he left the land of his birth and travelled to a land of opportunities—The United States of America.

Strange indeed is the fabric that the Weaver creates as time and space strands are woven together. Ever since I first came to these shores, I have used a blend of Eastern and Western philosophies that served me well except for the last few years—or perhaps I should say, in spite of the last few years. When I first met Gideon, my career and financial stability were being tested. I witnessed things that I had spent a lifetime building, slowly crumble. Even meeting God in the Big City had not prepared me for what was to follow. And what followed was nothing short of traumatic. Gideon was far from my mind when my car was repossessed. God seemed distant as creditors hounded me daily.

All that I had come to believe seemed to be destroyed. Anger, frustration, fear and unhappiness filled me to overflowing. Friends departed, leaving me to think that they were never friends in the first place. The two or three remaining ones helped as much as they could. Even brothers and sisters raised their voices in anger and disgust because of my inability to repay monies owed them. As days passed by, I was turning into an outcast. I remember sitting in the family room in the middle of winter with no heat as my wife and our two youngsters huddled over a small electric heater because the oil company had turned off our supply. Tears came to my eyes as I pleaded to no avail with the telephone company not to cut off our phone. Where was Gideon in the midst of this?

The questions weren't new and have been asked by thousands throughout the centuries. Why did I suffer so much? And if I had to suffer, why did my family and friends have to endure with me? All I had tried to do was to earn a decent living while treating my employees and others fairly. I had tried to live by the old injunction to "do justly, love mercy and walk humbly with God." But in spite of my efforts, it came crashing down. And fast. After the loss of the company, the comfort and security we had known as a family vanished as mist before the morning sun.

We lost our home and most of our possessions. We sold a few remaining pieces of furniture in order to buy groceries. One of the most difficult sacrifices I was forced to make was to give away "Rajah." He it was who had sat beside me as I conversed with Gideon. The question was not "Where was Gideon?" but, "Where was God?" Eventually we moved to another state in a final effort to start all over again.

And then, because he could not bear to see me suffer any longer, my father, descendant of Mahn Singh of Bharat land, passed away. Many were the sad moments I spent alone, but even so, a new understanding was dawning. On quiet evenings, as I drove from my job to my home, I could still hear his voice in my head.

One evening while driving home, I was thinking of how nice it would be to see Gideon again. Suddenly there was the sound of sirens. Looking into my rear view mirror, I saw the flashing lights of a state trooper about to pull me over. Not now, I thought. I could hardly afford the ticket. I must have been so absorbed in my thoughts that I exceeded the speed limit without knowing it. I pulled over to the side and fumbled through the papers in the glove compartment for my registration and license as I awaited the trooper. I looked up at the smiling face of a bearded man and almost dropped the papers in total surprise. "Gideon! You. . . . What. . . .

127

Why. . . . I mean. . . ." I could not continue. As his grin got bigger, I just stared at him in amazement.

"Well, at least say 'Hello'," he said.

"It's good to see you again, but why *this* way?"

"Just thought you could use a laugh and as I recall, you wanted to see me."

"Where did you get the car?"

As if he did this all the time, he calmly replied, "Created it." Ignoring his answer, I said, "I'd like to talk to you, but we can't stay here."

"That's why I came. I'll see you at ten tomorrow morning. Here's the address. We'll talk then." He handed me a piece of paper, gave me a slap on the shoulder, waved, turned around and walked back to his car. I looked at the address on the paper and then looked into the rear view mirror. He was gone, just like in the old days.

I could hardly contain myself as I drove the rest of the way home. Tomorrow I would see him again. I had many questions and this time I wanted answers. Tomorrow we shall see, I thought, as I pulled into my driveway.

CHAPTER

The morning finally arrived and I prepared for my meeting with Gideon. I was calm and composed yet there was a tinge of excitement that I could not hide. Because of my recent relocation, I was not familiar with many of the local streets so I pulled out a map of the immediate area. Having located the street, I went to the car and drove off.

At the designated address, I found a house. Walking up to the front door I anxiously rang the bell. A kindly-looking lady opened the door, smiled at me and said, "Please come in. You must be John. Gideon is expecting you." I thanked her and entered. I saw Gideon standing in the living room and walked over to greet him. He smiled and motioned for me to sit, which I did. Impatiently I waited. Nothing was said for a few moments as he sat. Sometimes, a few seconds could seem like an eternity.

"So how are you Gideon?" I finally asked. Anything to start a conversation, I thought.

"As usual, I am busy doing the things that need to be done," he replied matter-of-factly.

"Where were you during the past few years Gideon? I really needed help. Somehow I felt betrayed by you and even by God. Remember we met Him in the Big City? Or did we? Was it all nonsense? My tired mind playing cruel jokes on me?"

"No, not nonsense at all. Far from it. We were with you all the time. You were so blinded by what appeared to be happening to you that you weren't usually aware of our presence."

I almost shouted in anger but restrained myself. "Gideon, I have been and still am going through a forest of bewilderment and suffering. Lost my homes, my lands, my father, my company and most of my dignity and self-confidence. My wife was diagnosed as having cancer of the lymph nodes. Her parents are also being treated for cancer. There's no medical insurance. Hardly any money. I mean, how much can a person take? You don't know what it's like. . . ."

He interrupted me and said, "Yes, I know about all of that. But you gained strength, humility, wisdom and much more. Jim Elliot, one of earth's martyrs, once said, 'He is no fool who gives what he cannot keep to gain what he cannot lose.' The things that are important are still with you, even more so. Your dignity and self-confidence *are* still with you, but most of all you're regaining your sense of purpose."

"Sense of purpose about what?"

"About what you came here to do."

"Beats me. I have no idea what I came here to do, except, perhaps, to live and work and struggle until I die."

"Don't you have a feeling of something important that you must do in this lifetime?" he questioned.

"Oh sure, doesn't everybody? Anyway, why didn't you stay around and help when I needed it so much? Why didn't you tell me the things that were going to happen? You knew, didn't you?"

"Of course, I knew. But if I had told you about them, you probably would have given up and never reached this point."

"This point isn't much better than any of the other points along the way. As you can probably see, I don't earn enough money to even feed my family. It's all I can do to make ends meet. I've been struggling so hard, but there seems to be no progress. Why are bad things happening all the time, Gideon?"

"Bad things happen sometimes and good things can happen most of the time. It's how you look at it, John."

"There you go again, more riddles. Why don't you answer my questions? Have bad things ever happened to you?"

"Yes! Unpleasant things happened to me many times. But that was when I wasn't aware of who I was and of all the power I had at my command. It was only when I realized that I was both the giver and the gift, the creator and creation, the teacher and the student, that I learned to control the things that you call circumstances. Life then became much more fun. You think you have had tough times! Let me tell you about tough times!

"It was another time and another place, thousands of your earth years ago. It was the time of the Israelites and the Midianites. For some reason, the Midianites had conquered my people and we suffered terribly. For seven long years, as you count it, the Midianites would move across the land and destroy everything in their path. They took our sheep and cattle, our seed grain and all they could find. They killed our men, raped our women and destroyed our children. In spite of all that, we maintained our faith and kept on struggling.

"The Midianites would race over the land on fast-moving camels. They seemed numberless. Like locusts they came, destroying and laying waste the land until we had almost lost all hope. Now, my father Joash, had hidden some grain from the Midianites, and one evening, while it was not quite dark, I went near the wine press to thresh the grain so that we could get some food. Near the wine press was a giant oak tree. As I looked over to the oak tree, a man whom I had never seen before, stood up, walked over to me and raised his hand in greeting. Always mindful of spies, I was deathly afraid. But the face of the man was smiling and he seemed friendly enough. Perhaps, it was a messenger of God but then I was too frightened to ask.

"I stood there quivering as he said, 'Hello, you mighty man of valor, the Lord is with you.'

"I summoned up enough courage to ask a question, similar to the one you asked me earlier. 'If the Lord is with me, how come the Midianites destroy our land, kill our people and enslave us? What would it have been like if the Lord hadn't been with us?'

"The answer he gave did not make sense at the time: 'Go in your strength and save your people from the Midianites,' he said.

"I almost laughed, but seeing that the stranger was serious, I said, 'My clan is the weakest in Manasseh and I am the least important in my family. Please sir, how can I do anything?'

"The answer to my question is the same answer that I give to yours. The man said, 'The Lord will be with you and you shall smite the Midianites as one man.'

"You see, John, things were really bad. But that night, I got to thinking that if I really believed in myself and this power that is called God, I could do anything. The rest is recorded history, how, with only three hundred fighting men, we put the armies of Midian to flight. I then had all the wealth and power and happiness I could desire and lived to a ripe old age. When I died they, so to say, laid me to rest in the tomb of Joash my father at Ophra."

"You lived on earth before this time, Gideon?"

"Of course, I did. Many times. So did you."

"Do you remember all those times?"

"Only the ones I want to. But from each time, there was something important to learn. From that experience with the Midianites, I learned the importance of believing in myself and my God. I learned that no matter how bad things appeared to be, if you choose to change them and if you have a sense of purpose, you can overcome. You've had many lessons of this sort in other lives but you have forgotten them. It is in remembering and doing that you would find the answers to your present day problems."

"How do I go about trying to remember such things? And how can these things be true?"

"What do you mean by 'how can these things be true'? Can you tell me how a tree grows, or how a bird flies? Can you explain how the world works? Listen to your heart and soul in your quiet times and you'll see how much you remember and how much you really know. The door of the soul opens inward and meditation is the key that unlocks that door. You've taught many people how to meditate and yet, you do not heed your own instructions. 'Physician, heal thyself!'"

In a quiet voice I asked, "Gideon, what is happening to me?"

He looked at me with such kindly eyes and spoke in such understanding tones that I was somewhat embarrassed at the way I had been questioning him. "Look," he said, "what's happening to you is nothing that shouldn't be happening. You're discovering yourself again. You're going through a super laundromat—not a pleasant experience while it's happening, but when you come out, you are clean. Good gold must first go through the fire. You've been through a lot and suffered much. The time for tears is almost over. Don't give up now. You're almost there."

"Do you mean that all the events of the past few years had a purpose to them?

"Everything has a purpose even though you may not always be aware of it. The honeybee thinks that it only takes the nectar from the flower, yet, in doing so, it pollinates and so assists in the creation of fruits. There is an important reason for your being on earth. You must now start to use some of the learning you gleaned from your various experiences."

There was a knock at the door and in walked Marla, whom I had also not seen since the visit with God in the Big City. I stood up, smiled and took her extended hand. "John," she said, "it's so good to see you again. For a while there, we thought you weren't going to make it this time." She returned my smile and sat down next to Gideon. I again reseated myself.

Gideon then looked at Marla and asked, "How goes it with System 22?"

They both looked at me as Marla replied, "All

137

goes well. Perhaps John might enjoy a short visit there, don't you think?"

Gideon was serious as he said, "I don't know if he's ready yet, but I'll check with the Chief."

"What's System 22, Gideon?" I could feel something afoot.

"It's an entirely different system from the one to which you're accustomed. However, some preparations must be made before you're able to go there. In fact, a trip *has* been scheduled for you. We just have to double check to see if the time is right and if you're prepared. I'll let you know more about it soon."

I could see that further questions about System 22 would not be answered, so I didn't pursue the issue. I felt good seeing Gideon and Marla again. "Will I see you two more often?" I asked.

"More often than you may want to," Marla replied. "Gideon and I have been asked to give you all the help you need and to assist you in your growing process."

"That would really be a great help," I blurted out happily.

I left my other-worldly friends feeling that I had known them for ages and that I would see them again soon.

CHAPTER
14

A week had gone by since my last meeting with Gideon and Marla. Christmas was only a few days away and we, like many other families, were preparing for the occasion. Barely able to afford a tree, we settled for a sad-looking one and spent most of the weekend hanging ornaments, lights and decorations. Tired but pleased that we were able to make the most of what we had, I went to bed with the thought of getting a good night's rest.

I must have barely fallen asleep, when all of a sudden, I was wide awake again. Being awake this time, however, was somewhat different from other times. I seemed to be floating in the air. Disorienting as this appeared to be at first, I had a sense of expectancy, joy and freedom.

Looking down, I saw my body lying peacefully asleep between the sheets, yet, I was vibrantly awake, conscious and able to think. I peered around me and saw that the room was as I knew it. I also seemed to have a body but it was much lighter than the one to which I was accustomed. Perhaps I was dead, I thought, yet I felt more alive than I could ever remember. I was beginning to become afraid when a voice seemed to speak from within my head. "Look behind you, John," it said.

Immediately I turned around and saw both Gideon and Marla smiling at me. "Don't be afraid, my friend," said Gideon, "you're experiencing what's called an out-of-body situation. Your body is resting perfectly safe on the bed while you're here with us. In this state we're able to travel farther and faster, and of course, more efficiently than if you were in the physical body."

Still a bit scared, I asked Gideon, "Are you really sure that it's safe to be out of my body like this? I mean, isn't there a danger of my not being able to get back to it?"

"Not at all, John. You're perfectly safe. As a rule, most people do this during their sleep time. However, most don't remember it when they wake up in the morning."

"What's the point of this then? Why am I doing it?"

It was Marla who spoke next. I do not mean that a voice echoed throughout the room. In-

142

stead, I just seemed to hear her in my head. "Let's go to where it's somewhat more convenient and we'll tell you about the arrangements." She reached out and took my hand. Gideon grabbed the other one and all of a sudden, the three of us were flying, literally, through the roof. Over the house and above the trees we flew, until in a blur, we were standing under a tree in a wide open space. Beside the tree ran a gently-flowing stream. There was a bright moon above us and the sky was full of beautiful, fleecy clouds. There was neither a feeling of cold nor of heat—only a lovely, comfortable warmth. Behind me, stretching into infinity it seemed, was a narrow silver light, somewhat like a shining cord. Gideon, as if reading my thoughts, said, "We're speaking to you with our minds, John. Without the physical body, you have no need for physical voice or ears. You'll hear us, and we, you—as soon as thoughts are directed. Incidentally, that shining cord you see, is the silver cord that binds you to your physical body as it sleeps peacefully. Your 'Life Force' sustains it through the silver cord."

Marla interjected, "We use this method of travel when there are special things to be accomplished. This is a trail run for what you'll be doing in a few more days of earth time. Remember we mentioned System 22 during our last meeting? Well, your visit has been approved. We must tell you a little more about it, however, before we take you there. Somewhat like a mini-orientation."

"Well, I'm listening," I said, smiling.

"As you remember, you once visited the World Headquarters of G & M Enterprises," she continued. "There you met the Chief and had the pleasure of conversing with Him personally." I thought of how nice it would be to just lie in an easy chair listening to Marla. The thought had hardly occurred to me when I found myself reclining in a comfortable chair. Marla and Gideon were similarly positioned.

It was Gideon who spoke. "When you're out of your body as you are now John, your thoughts are materialized at the speed of light, or rather, at the speed of thought. The same thing could happen when you're in your body, of course, but then you have to take into account the concept called 'time'. So, controlling one's thinking is as essential here as it is there. As a man thinketh . . . remember?"

"Wow! What a fantastic place!" I shouted. "Could I think of all kinds of good things, fun things or whatever and would they appear?"

"Here, immediately. There, sooner or later. But appear, they will, as sure as day follows night. By the same token, however, if you think of unpleasant things, they too would be created. Just a universal law, John. Think and expect good and you get it. Think and expect bad and you get that, too. It is a double edged sword, you see. You can't get one without also having the ability to get the other, or else, where would your power of choice be? How could you exercise choice if you were only given one possible choice. Therefore, since the power of choice is one of the most important gifts from your Creator, you must have at least two choices and most times, many, many more. That's the fun and the complexity of it."

"Gee, Gideon, it's not as simple as I thought after all."

"Simple, it is. Easy, it's not. Most of your great teachers throughout history have spoken about the wisdom of controlling and choosing one's thoughts. Nevertheless, earth people still have much to learn."

Marla took up the conversation again. "When you travel through time and space on earth, you don't necessarily have to leave your physical body. Remember when you travelled to your old college and to the Ganges River? You took your body with you then because that was local travel. If you were, however, to travel to a different star system, it's much more efficient to do it this way, that is, without the physical earth body.

"We were discussing just such a situation a few moments ago. To go to the Head Offices of G & M Enterprises, you had no need for cosmic travel methods. However, System 22 is outside your star system and is the Universal Headquarters of the Chief. From that location, which is not really a place in the formal sense of the word, the entire universe is monitored and adjusted according to the thoughts and needs of its various inhabitants and life forms."

"Is it like a super headquarters from which the Almighty watches his universe?" I blurted out, still curious and excited.

"It's only headquarters for one universe. There are many universes and each one has its own support system. Ours and yours is System 22."

"How many universes are there altogether, Marla?"

"How many grains of sand are there in the desert? How many stars in the heavens?" she quickly asked in answer to my question.

We were all quiet for a while. I could "hear" the sound of the wind as it quietly moved through the leaves above me. "Then there must be other civilizations and people on other planets and Star Systems?" I asked.

"Yes, John," Gideon said. "There are many life forms in many universes. They were designed to live in harmony with one another. Similarly on earth, there are many life forms, each unique and having its own special place in the scheme of things. Just as the ant is able to co-exist with the elephant, mankind should be able to co-exist with one another and also with the various other life forms."

"Are some of the other civilizations more advanced than ours on earth, Gideon?"

"'Advanced,' is not the correct word. It would be more accurate to use 'aware,' but for illustrative purposes, let us use 'advanced.' Are there life forms on earth that are more advanced than others, more highly evolved, if you will? Of course, there are. So, similarly in the universe, there are some civilizations far more advanced than yours. Also, there are others far less evolved than earth people. Some are truly energy or light beings, having no need for a body as you know it. They're so aware of their infinite power that they create, out of pure thought, whatever they may need.

"Others are not as mature and still indulge in wars and other less evolved pastimes. But they are all children of the First Force and they're all striving in one way or another to achieve unity of purpose with their Creator. It's the same Creator who made you and us—The Chief Himself. We have instant access to Him."

"Would it be possible to see Him again soon? I mean, like I saw Him that time in the Big City?" I stammered.

"That's the purpose of the trip to System 22. In a few more days we'll make a trip to our Universal Headquarters. There the Chief will speak with you again and you'll be able to ask all the questions you have in mind. Think and reflect on what you have heard tonight. We must take you back now but when the time arrives for the journey, we'll let you know."

There was a hising sound and a flash of light. I turned over and was wide awake in bed. Marla and Gideon were gone. Of one thing I was sure, however; it was not a dream. I finally fell into a deep sleep.

CHAPTER

15

It was the day after Christmas. The morning was bitingly cold, but the golden rays of the sun bathed the trees in beauty far surpassing the words of poets or the paint of artists. Somehow, deep within me, I felt that this was to be the day for my visit to System 22. Yet nothing had happened to confirm the validity of my feelings.

Christmas day had been spent at home with the family. It was exciting to help my children with the setting up of their toys. I reflected on the days of my childhood and how I would wait with the greatest of excitement for Christmas day. With anxious fingers, I would rip off the wrappings from my gifts and delight myself with imaginary journeys to mysterious places. Christmas had not changed much with time, although, as I grew older, the spirit of Christmas had taken on a more commercial vein.

Today, however, Christmas was gone and it was time to return to the mundane world of work and money. The evening, I thought, should be a quiet and peaceful one. Not much occurred at the office and after a good dinner, some time with the family and a few household chores, I turned in for the night and fell asleep.

Without warning, it happened again. I was wide awake, looking once more at my body sleeping peacefully on the bed. Standing next to me were Marla and Gideon. "It's now time for us to go on a journey to System 22, John," said Gideon. "Your body will be at rest and perfectly safe while we are gone. Are you ready?"

"As ready as I ever will be," I replied, and without further ado, they each grasped one of my hands and we were off again. The same flying sensation occurred as before and then there was the feeling of falling. Almost immediately, we were standing in a brightly-lit room of enormous dimensions. The room was full of people who were strangers to me. They were talking to one another and occasionally glancing at various giant screens on the wall. Two younger men in their twenties walked over and greeted us. "Your turn will come shortly, Gideon," one of them said. They led us into what appeared to be a waiting room. It was tastefully decorated with expensive furnishings that seemed to be of the same type I saw in the offices of G & M Enterprises. We sat down and helped ourselves to some freshly brewed coffee. The thought came to me that even out of my body I enjoyed a good cup of coffee.

"Gideon, what is this place?" I asked.

"This is the first step in the 'translation' process from earth, so to say, to the heavens," he answered.

"What do you mean?" I was frankly puzzled.

"To reach System 22 from earth, there are several transfer points. Each earth being, who wants to go or is invited to visit, must first go through one of these transfer points. I don't know the exact reason why, but I understand that it has something to do with space-time coordinates. Purely technical, I guess. There are a number of such locations here on earth and a few of them are in this country. Right now, we're in an area you call Arizona. There are also transfer points in California, Virginia Beach and Massachusetts. Two new ones are in the process of being completed in Washington and Atlanta.

"Outside of this country, other such points are located, for example, in Canada, England, Australia and India. We chose Arizona for no particular reason except that we are familiar with it. You see, we have done this many times before. We could have gone to any of the other points, however.

"You'll notice that we all appear to have bodies. These bodies are mental ones, not physical ones, therefore they're not subjected to the time, space and density constraints, as are earth bodies. In fact, the earth body is a physical image of your mental body, somewhat akin to the way a picture shows an actual scene. From this transfer point, we'll go directly to System 22 where you'll meet some very interesting people and finally the Chief. I think they're ready for us. Let's go."

We stood up and walked over to one of the large screens, which was now glowing white. The two young men we'd met earlier waved us on. Gideon, Marla and I joined hands once again and before I could realize what was happening, we walked right through the screen on the wall.

There was immediate darkness, a sound not unlike music, then absolute stillness. I was no longer afraid, just curious. After what seemed to be an eternity, but in reality could not have been more than a minute, we emerged into another brilliantly lit room similar to the one we had just left. I turned to Gideon and said, "We didn't seem to have gone anywhere."

Smiling, he replied, "We're light years away from where we started."

A delegation was waiting for us—a group of friendly people who came forward and surrounded us. Looking at the faces around us, imagine my surprise when I saw my father almost the way I knew him back on earth. He looked into my eyes and smiled; I thought for sure that I was dreaming.

"No, you're not dreaming, son," he said to me.

"You're alive, Dad?" I said, more as a statement than a question.

"As alive, as I ever was or will be," he replied. He seemed to be happy and at peace. The crowd parted and Gideon and Marla, my Dad and I, walked across the room towards a large door. As we approached it, the door opened and we proceeded into a scene of remarkable beauty. Although we had left the transfer point at night, it was now full daylight. I decided to stop wondering about the mysteries of time and space.

Marla said, "We'll be back with you shortly, John," and she and Gideon vanished, leaving me alone with my Dad. I looked at this man who had raised me on earth and who had taught me much about life. He seemed to be surrounded by a faint silvery light.

"Sit down, son," he said as he pointed to a bench beneath a tree, "tell me how you've been."

"Well, to say the least, I've been having a rough time, Dad, but I am sure things will work out eventually. What's this place and what are you doing here?"

"This is a reception center for visitors from various parts of the universe. I'll be here for a while. I chose this assignment because of the opportunities for growth and learning, but it's also fun."

"Why did you leave us so suddenly on earth, Dad? Do you know how much all of us miss you, especially Mother? She speaks of you all the time. Recently, she was very ill, but she's doing

155

much better now. I think she misses you more than everyone else put together."

There seemed to be a moment of sadness in his eyes as he said, "It was time for me to go on." He was then quiet for a short while as if reflecting on what I had said. Then he continued, "I had completed as much of my earth work as I could accomplish and there was nothing else for me to do. From here, it's possible for me to help you and the others more than I was able to do there. I watch over your mother constantly. It will be quite some time, according to earth time, before she joins me. You have just started your work. All that came before was just a preparation. Your visit here is the next step and is like a graduation before going on to other, more involved things.

"I'll be with you whenever you need me. Just call me in your thoughts, like you used to call me aloud when you were a little boy. I'll answer and help you as I always tried to do. I never really left you at all; it only seems that way. Whenever you want to talk with me, find a quiet place for a short while, then close your eyes and see the old house in Guyana and the coconut palm growing by the edge of the little stream. I'll meet you underneath the tamarind tree and we can discuss whatever it is that's troubling you.

"There are others here who will be helping you, too. I know Gideon and Marla from many lifetimes. Then there is a group of three called the Companions. You see them often in your dreams. They always bring you valid information that very often you choose to ignore. They are your higher self—your guiding, knowing self. Everyone has several helpers. You are aware of some of yours, but most people on earth never discover the help that is available to them until they cross over to this side."

"Dad, I feel like crying. Not tears of sadness, but of joy."

"No need for tears, only joy. The Chief is all Love and Joy. You're the ones who believe that life is supposed to be a vale of tears and suffering. The Loving Force wants only for you that which you desire for yourselves. Some of you choose sadness and others of you happiness."

There was such a peace and joy surrounding us as we sat there. It seemed as though he had always been alive; that he had lived forever, this dad of mine whom I miss terribly during certain moments of my current earth life. I knew then that he had never really died and that I could always meet and see him whenever I wanted.

"Keep working, learning and growing, son," he continued. "Never give up. You've heard it said that when the student is ready, the teacher will appear. I believe that when the teacher is ready, the master will appear. You'll be meeting with the Chief soon. Then you should know that we're all one. You'll understand that you've never been separated from your Creator; that you and He are one.

"We must go now. Gideon and Marla are coming for you and the Lord is waiting."

Gideon and Marla reappeared as suddenly as they had left. My dad hugged me and then patted me on the back. Tears came to my eyes as he said good-bye. It was so good just to see him again. Of course, it was obvious now that he was not dead but transformed. As the butterfly lives within the caterpillar, so was he now a butterfly of the universe instead of a caterpillar of earth. "We wanted you to spend some 'time' with him, J.H.," Gideon said. "Now we'll go to see God— Whom we call—the Chief, First Cause, Creator and All That Is."

CHAPTER
16

Together, we walked along a lovely pathway in a garden of heavenly beauty. Flowers with the most delicate of forms blended their exotic scents to perfume the air with an ever so subtle fragrance. Surely, I thought, Eden must have been like this. Birds with brilliantly-colored plumes sang songs to warm the heart while butterflies painted the area with shades of every hue, creating a rainbow of colors.

We entered a nearby clearing into the midst of a garden party. A canopy of trees served as a tent and there were tables and chairs neatly set up. The sounds of talking and laughter rang out all around us. As we approached a table on the far side of the clearing, a stillness fell on the crowd. As I looked closer, I saw that there was

161

only one person sitting at that table. That person was God, looking just like I saw him in the Big City. "Hello, God, What are you doing sitting alone?" I asked.

"Sometimes it's lonely being God. Please sit," He said. We pulled up chairs and joined Him.

"Is this heaven, Lord?" I asked.

"No. This is not heaven. Heaven is neither here nor there. Let me assure you that heaven is closer to you than you may think. It is within you. All this comes from what is within you. Both heaven and hell are within your mind. All you have to do is choose which you would have."

"Bless you, Lord," was all that I could say. Realizing how ridiculously stupid I must have sounded, I quickly apologized. "Don't be embarrassed, John. It's generally the intent that's important," said God.

"Thank you, Sir," I replied. Marla and Gideon giggled in amusement at my situation.

"Why don't you say something, Gideon?" I asked, feeling at a loss for words.

"This is *your* party, John. We're celebrating your visit and life itself."

Looking at God, I said, "Lord, I am so happy to be here. When I return home, I'll spend my life building You a temple where others and I can worship and praise You."

"That's very kind of you," He said, "but whatever gave you the idea that I dwell in temples and that I want to be worshipped and praised? Look, I really get bored with this praise thing.

Instead of building me a temple, why don't you feed the hungry, help the poor, heal the sick and teach those who want to learn? Wouldn't that be of much more use than a temple?"

God continued speaking. "I've invited a number of others to be our guests and to join in our celebration. Let me introduce some of them." He stood up and pointed to various tables, calling names. "There is Abraham, Moses, Annabelle Thomas and Krishna. And over on the other side Rama, Mohammed, Gautama and Jacob. To our right, under that oak tree you can see Jesus, Peter, Paul, Elizabeth the First, Joan of Arc, Gandhi and Mary of Magdala. Sitting with them are Martin Luther King, Confucius, Jennifer Thompson, Benjamin Franklin and Joseph Rigby. These are some of my children, my friends and helpers. After tea, you should go around and meet them and some of the others."

"How can all these be at the same party, Lord?" I asked, "I mean, Krishna and the Buddha conversing with Mohammed and Jesus? And who are Joseph, Jennifer and Annabelle?"

"They were all created in my image. Each is as important as the other. The famous names, you recognize. The other three, though not spoken of in your history books, are quite as dear to me. They were just simple folks on your earth, each one trying to fulfill his or her mission. This is a cooperative universe, not a competitive one, John. For someone to be richer, another does not have to be poorer. For you to be healthy, no one has to be sick. There is enough and more than enough for everyone. In the game of life, all can win and all can receive prizes."

"Is this all a dream and will I forget when I wake up?"

"No, this is not a dream. And yes, you will forget some, but not all. The important things will stay in your memory for the rest of your earth life. Tolerance, harmony and understanding, these are some of the important things. Learn to understand yourself and you will find it easy to understand all else.

"Earth life appears to be so difficult at times for those who are there. Yet there's no need for suffering and pain. Suffering should only teach you that you didn't really have to suffer in the first place. Help is always available if you choose to ask for it, so ask, seek and knock. You have helpers on many dimensions who are more than willing and able to help you when you're caught in a difficult situation. When you need help, ask for it and of course, I, too, am always there to assist you."

I interrupted God at this point. "Lord, You say we should ask for help, but I've asked many times and yet it seemed that there wasn't any answer. I seemed to have been worse off than before asking. How do You explain that?"

"It's very simple indeed. Many times you ask without believing that you will get an answer. Sometimes you do not think that you deserve an answer. At others times, you're pleading and begging and talking so much that you can't hear the answer.

"Then there are those times when you are like your son who has just broken his toy locomotive. He asks you to fix it for him but he holds on to it and will not give it to you. In fact, he even tells you how to fix it. You want a problem solved? Then don't hold on to it. Release it to me and go about your work. Let go and let God."

"Do You mean it's that simple? That makes sense though. I think I'll try it," I said.

"You always have enough to do what has to be done—more than enough, actually, to take care of all your needs and wants. Sometimes you go through trials, but that's only to strengthen parts of you and to give you a deeper understanding. You're never alone. I am with you always. When you're down in the arena and your face is in the dust and the crowds are booing, don't give up. When they laugh at you and ridicule you and say all manner of vile things against you, don't give up. When you feel the boot of your opponent on your neck, when you feel that life is not worth living any longer, remember this . . . it's not over yet. Don't let go of hope. Hope keeps mighty big company with faith and love. Get a faith-lift if you must and do not abandon hope."

"You say that You're always with me and Your other children. Yet, I don't always see You as I see You now. In fact, I had to travel through transfer points on earth to get here. Gideon told me that we are somewhere on the third star of the Aldebaran System. Do You know how far I figure we must be from earth, Lord? Very far. If You are always with me, why do I have to travel so far to see You? How can You hear when I call?"

"Precisely the point I want to make clear, John. You didn't have to go through transfer points or travel great distances to see me. You believed that was the only way to do it, so, we accommodated your beliefs. As you believe, so it is. You are on Aldebaran and you are on earth. You are everywhere and nowhere. Your essence and nature span the universe itself and like me, you can be everywhere and everywhen. Even when you seem to be 'nowhere' you are still 'now-here.'

"Beliefs are extremely important. You think that you believe what you see. Instead, you see what you believe. Instead of trying to 'set' things right, try to 'see' them right and then they'll automatically be set right. See your problems and challenges through me instead of seeing me through them.

"You tend to think of yourselves as a people of beginnings and endings. And yet there is neither. That which you love will continue forever just as surely as that which you hate. Do away with that which you don't want by ceasing to hate and resist it. There is only one power and one force in the universe and I AM THAT. I

166

created you in my image and likeness so YOU ARE THAT.

"The power to heal and prosper you, to guide and help you is not in the skies. It is and has always been within you. I am within you. All you have to do is to become aware that I am there. There is mountain-moving power in each and every one of my children. You are *a part* of me and yet, at times, you think yourselves *apart* from me. You are made as I am. That which I do, you can also do. You are all co-creators with me.

"You wonder about 'prayer' at times and think that it must be magical. There's no magic in it. It's a method I gave to you so you could reach me at anytime you desired. It was designed to bring you to the realization that you should be aware of me all your life. Prayer does not change me, it changes you. Use it as it was originally taught. Come first to yourself and then you'll find that you have come to me.

"You are a child of the King, a prince of the realm. All of you are children of the King and thus princes and princesses. You just have to be aware of your birthright to understand the so-called mysteries of life. Look around at the trees, the mountains and the skies. You should know that long before they were, you have been and long after they are gone, you shall continue to be."

God continued. "Perhaps, it would help you to understand better if you walk around a bit and talk to some of my other children here. Many of them have gone through a lot worse than you have and yet they were victorious. Enjoy the party, John. Life is really a celebration."

Listening to God speak again was an experience never to be forgotten. Marla, Gideon and I walked over to various tables and spoke with some of the people. It was indeed delightfully refreshing to converse with the great personalities of all time. I walked over to Jesus who was having a conversation with the Buddha. "Pardon me for interrupting," I said, "Do you have much in common?"

"More than most people on earth would like to believe," said the Buddha.

"Lord Christ, could You tell me why You had to die on a cross?" I asked.

"I didn't have to die, not on a cross nor anyplace else. As you can see, John, I am far from dead. My followers, if you look over there," he pointed to Peter and Paul, "were a group of pretty somber folks and I had to make quite an impression on them. I had to make sure that they got the message and were going to teach others about the laws of life. They quickly forgot the 'miracles and parables' but my so-called 'death and resurrection' gave them the impetus needed to spread the teaching. Naturally, after all was said and done, somewhere along the line their followers got everything mixed up. They started worshipping me instead of teaching and living what I'd taught them. The same thing happened to my friend here, Prince Gautama, or as he's more commonly known, the Buddha."

The Buddha took up the conversation. "When I first started to understand the laws of the universe, I was sitting under a Bodhi tree. I thought how excellent it would be to share what I had found. But those who came after me interpreted and misinterpreted what I tried to say. You cannot even recognize some of the things I taught them. Well, there will be others of us who will keep trying. To raise ourselves higher, we must endeavor to raise the consciousness of the entire human race."

"Will you still help us then?"

"I, Jesus and others, will always be with you to help if you call upon us. Just believe that we are with you, and bingo, there we are. No need for meaningless sacrifices and rituals. You have direct access to the Chief. Direct access to any of us. Only believe and know that this is so."

Confucius came over and joined in the conversation. "Listen, John," he said. "We all have been trying to say the same thing for ages. The Buddha's message was love. Jesus exemplified this the best. He taught about love. Love yourself. Love your neighbor. Remember the golden rule? Love is the most powerful force in your universe. The whole thing is very simple. Earth people must learn that they are all shipmates on the common voyage of life and that they *cannot* sink their shipmates without sinking themselves. Ask Gandhi over there and he'll tell you. You must love without expecting anything in return. Ask God. He loves us exactly as we are. You should try 'love' sometimes. Work on love, John. Don't try to teach people how to love. Just show them by example."

God walked over to us while tea was being served. Next to Him was a tall, remarkable looking fellow. "John," God said, "I want you to meet Lord Michael. You and your legends know him as the archangel, Michael. Don't be surprised that he hasn't any wings. He only uses wings when there's a need for such appearances." I bowed with reverence and thought to myself that it wasn't possible for God, His angels and others to be speaking to me. How can this be, I thought, I, a relatively insignificant human being.

Immediately God answered my unspoken question. "I speak to all," He said, "and I speak through all. Do you see Peter over there? They used to call him Simon. I spoke to him and through him I spoke to many others. He was just a common fisherman, you say? But what a fisherman. When he became aware of my presence through the teachings of Jesus, he spoke in thunder tones of truth. How about Paul? At one time they called him Saul of Tarsus. He was formally educated, having studied under Gamaliel at the Sanhedrin in Jerusalem. Gautama was a prince on your earth. Even Mary of Magdala heard and understood me.

"Look at Mohandas Karamchand Gandhi. See

170

how quietly he sits? A simple lawyer you say he was? A lawyer, yes, but much more aware of universal laws than petty, man-made ones. Laws were made for man, not man for laws. He spoke of non-violence and love and millions of people listened to him. And Jesus? He was born but the son of a carpenter and yet hundreds of millions of you believe in him. I wish more of you would believe in what he said. I speak to you and I speak through you. We speak for each other.

"Speak the truth wherever you may find it. Seek the truth wherever it is to be found. Don't confuse facts with truth. Facts may not even be facts at all. Most times, they're just opinions. Facts are relative. Truth is absolute. Instead of trying to force your facts on others, help them to find truth for themselves.

"You're all brothers and sisters on a common journey towards your true potential. You have the power of God with you. You've always had it. You're as free as you ever will be. If your experience seems to be lacking in this freedom, it's only because you have been fettered in chains of your own forging. Lift up your head and look. See with your true eyes and you'll never again be in bondage to yourself or to another. My will for you is really your own will for yourself.

"All powers in heaven and earth have been given to you. All, except one. You do not have the power to destroy life, even your own. No one has that power. It is mine and mine alone. Life is my greatest gift to you and I permit no one to destroy it. Even when it appears that life has been destroyed, it's only an illusion you see.

"There are those who say that they have found me and rejoice in their finding. They have only found themselves, for I've never been lost. You, my son, are as valid as I am. When you can say to yourself, 'I and my Father are One,' then will you be a master of the universe. You see, I am *you* in spirit as much as *you* are me in becoming."

God stopped speaking. The party grew quiet. Gideon and Marla smiled at me. All of a sudden, I was alone. But there was a tremendous sense of power and knowing within me. A voice, still and small, spoke in my head, "We are one . . . all in one and one in all. The good that you do, you do for yourself. The evil that one does is his alone."

I was startled to find myself in my bedroom wide awake. It is now late and I have learned much. Perhaps, I shall again see Gideon and Marla, but now I know that forever and ever, they and those I love, will always be with me; that God has always been, is, and always will be with me.

It was time to be about my work, to seek the bliss beyond the now. This is not an ending. It is not even the beginning of an ending. It is but simply a beginning and so be it.

AUTHOR'S NOTE

Perhaps in reading the preceding pages, you have acquired a greater insight into the "Larger Thought of God." Some things may have struck a harmonious chord within you and others may have served to disturb you. In either case, I wish you a joyful and "learningful" journey through this seemingly confusing path we call "daily living."

Books from America's most acclaimed outdoorsman

TOM BROWN, JR.

His celebrated Tracking, Nature and Wilderness Survival school are proof that Stalking Wolf, an ancient Apache, knew what he was doing when he took a New Jersey boy under his wing and passed on an art more ancient than mankind.